Global Uprising

Confronting the Tyrannies
of the 21st Century

Stories from a
New Generation of Activists

NEVA WELTON AND LINDA WOLF

PHOTOGRAPHY BY LINDA WOLF

NEW SOCIETY PUBLISHERS

Cataloguing in Publication Data:
A catalog record for this publication is available from the National Library of Canada.

Cover design by Diane McIntosh. Cover photo: Agence France-Presse.

Printed in Canada by Friesens.

New Society Publishers acknowledges the support of the Government of Canada through the Book
Publishing Industry Development Program (BPIDP) for our publishing activities, and the assistance of the
Province of British Columbia through the British Columbia Arts Council.

BRITISH
COLUMBIA
ARTS COUNCIL
Supported by the Province of British Columbia

Paperback ISBN: 0-86571-446-0

Inquiries regarding requests to reprint all or part of *Global Uprising* should be addressed to New Society
Publishers at the address below.

To order directly from the publishers, please add $4.50 shipping to the price of the first copy, and $1.00 for
each additional copy (plus GST in Canada). Send check or money order to:

New Society Publishers
P.O. Box 189, Gabriola Island, BC V0R 1X0, Canada

New Society Publishers' mission is to publish books that contribute in fundamental ways to building an
ecologically sustainable and just society, and to do so with the least possible impact on the environment, in
a manner that models this vision. We are committed to doing this not just through education, but through
action. We are acting on our commitment to the world's remaining ancient forests by phasing out our paper
supply from ancient forests worldwide. This book is one step towards ending global deforestation and
climate change. It is printed on acid-free paper that is **100% old growth forest-free** (100% post-consumer
recycled), processed chlorine free, and printed with vegetable based, low VOC inks. For further information,
or to browse our full list of books and purchase securely, visit our website at: www.newsociety.com

NEW SOCIETY PUBLISHERS   www.newsociety.com

Contents

Acknowledgments

A book like *Global Uprising* is possible only with the support of many generous, passionate, committed, and talented people. We deeply thank Forrest Hawes, Jimmy Mateson, and Phil Lindsey for inviting us to participate in the early planning meetings for the WTO protests in Seattle. We'll never forget the many midnight discussions, personal revelations, and joy of being in community with three inspired brothers. Big hugs go to LaMer Riehle for spending innumerable hours transcribing tapes and working with us as we passionately determined the flow and order of the stories; we so appreciate your vibrant enthusiasm, sharp intellect, and moral support. Great thanks go to Elizabeth and Gifford Pinchot for their friendship and unfailing support; and to Anita Roddick, Joel Solomon, the Tides Foundation, Dr. Frank Ochberg, and our Bainbridge Island and Seattle communities for sponsoring our West Coast and East Coast research trips.

Thanks to Jessica Ziakin, Carla Schmidt, Heather and Jenni Wolf-Smeeth, and Tamara Smith for additional transcribing and office support that came just at the right time. And Josh Dzzzz, for all the dinners and clean kitchens.

A project like this requires ongoing contextual support and analysis of the many complex issues represented in the book. We are very grateful to the individual members of our Advisory Board, who provided emotional, spiritual, and intellectual guidance: Jia Ching Chen, China Galland, Tad Hargrave, David Korten, Paul Rogat Loeb, Elise Miller, Ocean Robbins, Anita Roddick, John Sellers, Starhawk, Coumba Touré, Justine Toms, and Howard Bloom, who cracked the title!

We extend our gratitude also to our friends and colleagues for their support: Vicki Robin and Monica Wood, Barbara Larsen, Audrey Watson, Lucy Leu, Roberta Wilson and Jeff Moore, Lisa and Norm Down, Colette Dewitt, Leigh and Van Calvez, Carol Shakow, Wende and Richard Jowsey, Malika Sanders, Monique Waugh, Nancy Davis, Dwight Wilson and Deborah Davis, Doña and Charles Keating, Alex Burns, Alan Crutchfield and Bryn Barker, and everyone at Ruby's of Bainbridge Island.

Along the way, we asked many organizations for assistance and scholarships to their trainings and youth conferences. For their support we thank the awesome folks at Bioneers, YES! Youth for Environmental Sanity, Ruckus Society, 21st Century Youth Leadership Movement, New Roadmap Foundation, the Youth Summit on Globalization sponsored by Amnesty International and the Sierra Club, Positive Futures Network, the

Conference for Organized Resistance, Mary Bull and the Gapitistas, Jennifer Kloes and Global Youth Connect, Barbara Briggs and the National Labor Committee, Kyle Kajihiro and the Hawaiian American Friends Service Committee, Global Exchange, Public Citizen, Council of Canadians, Vote Nader Committee, the International Forum on Globalization, disinfo.com, Third Wave Foundation, and Media Island International. We are extremely grateful to Janette Reynolds, for the equipment donations we received from Epson USA and photographic services from Panda Lab in Seattle. Special thanks to the Daughters Sisters Project (www.daughters-sisters.org) for sponsoring *Global Uprising* and to Forrest Hawes for keeping www.youthactivism.org and www.globaluprising.net alive and vital.

The journey of researching, interviewing, writing, and editing has been as meaningful as the final published work, thanks to the talented staff at New Society Publishers. To Chris and Judith Plant: We are very grateful for the extraordinary opportunity to have worked with you both. Thank you for your friendship, warmth, expertise, and guidance along the way. To our editor, Audrey Keating: We are so grateful to you for staying on the phone with us for hours, always with encouragement, good ideas, enthusiasm, and insight; and for spending so many days and nights editing at the end to make sure we reached our deadline. We would not have been able to find the river of stories without you. Also, thanks to our designers Greg Green and Nancy Pagé for their remarkable job in presenting this nonlinear material in a linear form, and to Lisa Garbutt, Jack Howell, and Justine Johnson for getting *Global Uprising* into so many hands. To all our friends at NSP: We are incredibly fortunate to have you as allies!

To the many unknown comrades who helped our call for entries travel around the world on the Internet at least 25 times, thank you. We received stories and inquiries from every inhabited continent in the world. To those of you whose stories we could not publish in this book (due simply to lack of space): Your words inspired, informed, and energized us. We are pleased to be able to share many of these stories on the website: www.youthactivism.org. We hope that people will continue to send us stories, ideas, photos, poems, and analysis of critical issues for future inclusion.

To the contributors of *Global Uprising*: No words can express our gratitude for the strength and wisdom you bring to the world and to this book. Thank you for sharing your stories and for trusting us with your precious memories, experiences, and truths. We believe that not only will your actions change the world, but that the words you have shared here will also contribute to the rise of civil society and a true, living democracy.

Introduction
Ain't No Power Like the Power of the People

What is it that gets inside and moves us and suddenly we are up on our feet, standing firm for something we believe in? What is it that gives us the juice to stay up all night and strategize a campaign, paint protest signs, make giant puppets and spend hours sending emails, licking stamps, answering phones, or leafleting in front of stores? What is the ineffable quality that triggers our resistance, resolve, and courage — that holds us up when we face a line of riot police, hang from the side of a freeway, lie down in front of a logging truck, start a lawsuit, give a speech, blow the whistle?

We believe it is a primal instinct that rises up when enough is enough, when injustice can no longer be tolerated, when the hidden must come to light. Born of outrage and fueled by hope and compassion, it is a palpable sensibility that moves us to risk our comfort, our bodies, our lifestyles, and even our lives, because we know there is nothing to do but to struggle for what is right.

This spirited impulse has infused generations of activists throughout history and is bringing hundreds of thousands of people to the streets in a worldwide movement marked by mass demonstrations against corporate globalization and the governing economic bodies that threaten the basis of democracy. A new generation of activists is also speaking out and joining people who struggle, as they have for years, to eradicate war, hunger, poverty, racism, sexism, heterosexism/homophobia, and the increase in social, economic, environmental, and political injustice.

Global Uprising begins with the historical events of November 1999, when more than 50,000 people and 700 organizations demonstrated in Seattle (and in solidarity events around the world) to protest the

World Trade Organization's (WTO's) corporate agenda and the new round of closed-door trade talks that govern the global economy. Students, teachers, farm workers, factory and steel workers, feminists, environmentalists, scientists, spiritual leaders, gay rights activists, animal lovers, magic workers, shopkeepers, friends and families all took to the streets for the sake of global justice. Amidst tear gas and rubber bullets, in blockades, and chanting, we stood together for fair labor standards, environmental protection, public health, and for life-centered, democratic values over the perpetual money-first ethics of our current system.

When it was over, we stood in the aftermath of a ravaged city. We sat in jail cells refusing to give our names; compiled eyewitness accounts; cleaned the streets; and traveled home to other cities, towns, and countries, knowing we had come together for a purpose and had succeeded. We had shut down the WTO, if only for a while, and had lifted the veil of secrecy that shrouds the undemocratic institutions that govern economic globalization.

The 'Battle in Seattle' was not the start of a new social movement nor would it be the end. It was a soul force — a hope-filled turning point that affirmed, united, and rejuvenated activists everywhere. It was a coming-out party for a new movement of citizen power. It was a magical and potent time of global solidarity that created new social forums, re-inspired civil society, educated and shaped a whole new generation of activists, and challenged core movement practices such as tactics, organizational diversity, and leader-ship. Issues of racism, sexism, classism, ageism, heterosexism/homophobia, and national-ism came to the fore as people analyzed the successes and failures of Seattle. The need to address this 'web of oppression' is fundamental to real social change.

Since Seattle, hundreds of thousands of people have continued to mobilize all over the world. International mass actions in Melbourne, Australia; Washington, DC, Philadelphia, and Los Angeles, USA; Prague, Czech Republic; Nice, France; Quebec City, Canada; Gothenburg, Sweden; and Genoa, Italy have shaken the political and economic establishment. In November 2001, the WTO is holding its bi-annual ministerial conference in Doha, Qatar — a state that has scant respect for freedom of speech or assembly and little tolerance for dissent. Though Qatar is relatively inaccessible, international activists will be holding demonstrations and converging on regional centers worldwide.

As the movement for global justice grows, the stakes have become higher, violence has escalated, and repressive forces have become more aggressive. Still, significant demonstrations and actions of all sizes, rarely reported, are happening daily in cities and countries all over the world. Tree sits, popular education campaigns, boycotts, sit-ins, cyber activism, cooperative living, guerrilla actions, political theater, hip-hop concerts, union organizing, teach-ins, human rights abuse documentation, nonviolent civil disobedience, and leadership training are but some of the ways in which dedicated individuals are confronting the tyrannies of the 21st century.

As planners, participants, and witnesses of those transformative days in November 1999, we wanted to know more about the people behind the blockades, lock-downs, and banner-hangs. We wanted to know about the struggles of those who traveled halfway around the world to march in the streets of Seattle and about those who couldn't, but whose lives are dedicated to peace and justice. As social activists, we wanted to document and publish accounts of this powerful time of uprising — accounts we knew would not be reported on the evening news.

As you read *Global Uprising*, you will discover (as we have) a newfound strength in the youth movement and a resounding hope in longtime activists, who feel encouraged and inspired by the courageous acts of young activists today. Whether you are a seasoned activist or are just learning, these stories will have an impact on the way you think and feel about your place in civil society and in the hard realities of our time. You'll meet Neta Golan, the Israeli woman who uses herself as a human shield to protect her Palestinian friends' olive trees from being destroyed by the Israeli Army. You'll find out how Coumba Touré's vigorous public education campaign reversed a *fatwa* (religious indictment) against a Muslim woman who had made a video critical of female genital mutilation. And you'll read of Luis Sánchez, whose tireless work as a high school teacher and organizer has brought attention to the systemic unfairness in the education system for youth of color.

These stories and others will move you; challenge you; shock, anger, and educate you. Most importantly, we hope they will inspire you to action. As the late Rev. Martin Luther King, Jr. said, "No social advance rolls in on the wheels of inevitability. It comes through the tireless efforts and persistent work of dedicated individuals." Individuals such as Julia Butterfly Hill, who demonstrated phenomenal courage as she sat for two years in a 1000-year-old tree to protest old-growth logging; or Sonia Beatriz Lara, who bravely helped organize the first union in the free trade zone in El Salvador.

Global Uprising also features the persistent efforts of adult activists who share the wisdom that comes from a lifetime of committed action. J.L. Chestnut imparts hope for radical change through his personal experiences of the civil rights movement; Noam Chomsky clarifies the threat of economic globalization as the major issue of our time; and Vandana Shiva tells of the devastating effects of corporate agri-farming in India.

Together, the stories represent the currents that make up the 'many movements within a movement.' Such fluidity makes the task of organizing the book a difficult one. The material itself resisted division into categories such as social, political, economic, or environmental activism. Since two of the hallmarks of modern-day activism are its diversity and its unlikely, nontraditional associations and collaborations, we did our best to present a flow that speaks to the complexity and richness of these profound and exciting times.

Global Uprising does not have chapters. Instead, we have chosen to use various design elements to help you navigate. As you thumb through the book, you will notice tabs that are titled Context, Tactics, Mentor, Witness, Organization, or Resources. Whether you are reading from cover to cover or dipping in here and there, use these tabs to orient yourself to the book's diversity of material. Many of the pieces have websites associated with them; these appear under a LINKS icon and offer a quick jumping off point if you want to find out more. You will also notice short quotations in the margins; these appear as Another Voice and are the thoughts or observations of individual activists. Our intent in organizing the book this way is to have both its content and design reflect the fluid cohesion that is the essence of global activism.

The mainstream media would like to simplify, diminish, or gloss over the importance of such mass efforts to speak out as occurred in Seattle, Quebec City, and Genoa. But each and every person in the streets represents the daily work of activists everywhere who are working tirelessly to make this world one that works for all. Worldwide, people are rising up, telling powerful global institutions and players, "Ain't no power like the power of the people, and the power of the people won't stop."

September 10, 2001, Bainbridge Island, Washington

Stay in touch at www.globaluprising.net

This book is dedicated to furthering human understanding & compassion, the necessary ingredients for waging peace instead of war.

Shannon Service

RICHARD SERVICE

▶ 1.

Our Sacred Duty

Exposing the Spectacle of Global Consumer Culture

| SHANNON SERVICE |

It's amazing how short the distance is between the smooth interior of a shell and a freeway wall. Standing on the beach a few years ago, running my finger along the silvery wall of a seashell, my ideas of what is valuable and worth preserving suddenly shifted. I realized very clearly, in a moment, that the delicate and beautiful sea form in my hand was considered valueless in our market economy. In fact, everything I held to be important — from clean air to ancient trees — fell outside of the current system of accounting. I made a decision on that beach to consciously value things based on their intrinsic beauty and not their sticker price. In a few years, that simple decision would send me rappelling over the edge of a freeway wall in Seattle to hang a banner protesting the World Trade Organization.

Growing up with Generation X meant growing up in a world where everything was for sale. As a child, I saw America's grade schools fill with advertisements. In high school, I lived under Pepsi's threat to project their logo on the moon. In college, malls were constructed on our campuses, and it became difficult to find even a kid's softball game that wasn't corporate sponsored. The traditional names for our nation's ballparks, like Candlestick and Fenway, gave way in rapid succession to names like Network Associates Coliseum, Pacific Bell Park, and Coors Field.

By the time I graduated from Mount Holyoke College, I had the option of living in Celebration, Florida, the town owned by the Disney Corporation. Everywhere I turned, I was encouraged to consume my identity and even my liberation, in the form of this new computer or that new SUV. Want to think different? Buy a Macintosh. Want to embrace diversity? Buy Benetton. Tired of the two-party system? Buy a Nissan. This onslaught of advertising narrowly defined my ideas of the human experience, until my future seemed to be nothing more than a series of bigger and bigger purchases. It also created an overwhelming feeling that without corporate support, our schools, our national pastimes, and our communities would fall apart. I began to understand that globalization is founded on the myth that the Earth and people's labor do not provide for us — corporations do.

Corporate culture perpetuates the myth, by telling us repeatedly that being human is about skating along in baby blue leather pants, watching *Friends*, and upgrading our software. The hidden world that lies behind the labels and inside the Happy Meal is a world we are always carefully sheltered from. Beneath the spectacle of global consumer culture lies an underbelly of clearcut rainforests, forced dislocation, burgeoning sweatshops, food insecurity, a booming skin trade, and the use of military force to protect corporate interests.

I saw the dark underbelly very clearly a couple of years ago, when I spent a night in a bar in the Philippines watching 12-year-old girls pole dance to bring money in for their families. The girls were selected by middle-aged American businessmen, who paid for them in cash at a register before taking them out of the bar. One by one, the men would come in, sit at the bar, and watch the girls dance. One by one, the girls would come out and move mechanically through routines they had repeated every night for months. The thumping bass of mid-80s techno-music mingled with the continuous sound of coins dropping into the cash register by the door.

All the justifications for the global economic interests that had ripped many of these girls' families off their land and forced their daughters into the global skin trade ran through my head: "Globalization is good for the poor. Globalization will improve the lives of women and children." (Music thumps, the register opens and closes.) "Globalization will improve human rights conditions in all nations. We're creating a global village." (The men reach for their wallets.) "Globalization will be the rising tide that lifts all boats. Globalization is inevitable; we can't turn back now." (A girl follows a 60-year-old man out into the warm island night.)

As with many nations, the history of the Philippines is a long story of repeated colonization and exploitation. Today, it is once again caught in a system that commodifies its rainforests and its women for the material and sexual pleasures of the global North. Girls are bought and sold between business meetings and beers, without a trace of deeper consideration. In our commodity-driven economy, Filipino girls become just another consumable in the global marketplace.

An enormous tension developed within me between my experience of all that is necessary and beautiful in this world and my role in a global capitalist system that is inherently destructive and denies our basic connections to each other and the Earth. I knew that if we could all clearly see the connections between the trade laws established by institutions like the WTO and their impact on people and ecosystems, Americans would join the global uprising against economic colonialism, and the system would break down.

In fall of 1999, a few days prior to the WTO protests in Seattle, my friend Leonie and I stood on the top of a freeway wall on Interstate 5, getting ready to rappel down. As we slid into our harnesses and prepared the ropes, a huge sense of relief washed over me. Hanging the banner was not just about bringing attention to the injustices of the WTO in the hopes of creating a more life-centered and compassionate trade system. It was about freeing myself from the institutions of fear that preserve the current systems by keeping us docile. It was about remaining true to my promise to value life above profit and about committing fully to creating more space for resistance and spontaneity in the world. I no longer feared being arrested. I no longer feared jail. Leonie and I went over the freeway wall and into a life that was a little freer, more profound, and fun.

Within minutes, several police cars had shut down two lanes of I-5 in the middle of rush hour. The SWAT team was called in. A black helicopter hovered overhead. As the sirens blared and the chopper circled, we sang and dangled in the rain. Lights from the backed-up cars stretched deep into the horizon. The stars came out and the moon rose above the buildings of Seattle. Taking the whole scene in — activists playing music in the streets around us, cars honking their support below, police standing around in bunches, the moon shining up above — I understood what it means to me to be an activist. Being an activist simply means that I am willing to risk my physical comfort for the possibility of bringing beauty and compassion into the world.

Since Leonie and I dropped that banner on I-5, I've shed many of the illusions of activism that I once held. I now see that it is

Shannon Service is a founding member of The Direct Action Network and is currently a climb trainer for The Ruckus Society. She lives in Boulder, Colorado, where she directs Rocky Mountain Media Watch and works for Free Speech TV.

LINKS

www.bigmedia.org

part of our sacred duty as humans to be an essential part of the complex and gorgeous systems that generate and regenerate life. I see how we, the generations, revolve into and out of each other like glass doors, and how it is our deepest honor to consider those connections before we make decisions. I've shed the illusion that struggling for social and ecological justice somehow makes me special — it only makes me human. Most importantly, I see how doing this work has begun to extricate me from the trappings of consumer culture and helped me to create a more connected life that is based on what I truly value. I'm beginning to shed the illusion that I'm saving the Earth — from that very first moment on the beach, the Earth has been saving me.

▶ 2.

Taking Responsibility
Waking Up to the Connection Between Privilege and Poverty

| ROLI KHARE |

"*Chai! Chai! Garam chai!!*" Man, it must be morning. Otherwise I wouldn't have this old man practically tearing my eardrum out. The train has come to a complete stop, and my mom and brother decide to buy some food at the station in Fatehpur Sikri, for we have about another ten hours to go on the train. I glance at the container of Danish cookies my mom has brought for us. In fact, there is an entire bag full of American food, in case we are not able to adjust to the cuisine of India. Unfortunately, I have gotten so sick of eating Banana Granola Crunch, fruit snacks, and Danish cookies. But hell, it's morning and I'm hungry.*

Glancing outside, I notice a bustling society within the station. You have many coolies (bellboys), ready to take your luggage anywhere. You have taxi drivers, trying to persuade you that they can get you anywhere in the city in less than ten minutes (with traffic), and that they'd charge you the lowest price in town. You have people frantically going in and out of the trains, saying their last good-byes, wishing well, wiping away their tears.

Ten minutes and still no sign of my mom or brother. Munching on the stale sugar cookies, I notice a boy my age

▲

Roli Khare

approaching me. "Didi, mein bahut book huin. Mujay kuch kanay ko do." (Sister, I am very hungry. Can you give me some food?)

I have seen and interacted with the homeless, the poverty-stricken, and beggars, both at home and in other countries. But there is something strikingly different with this encounter. It is the first time I have looked straight into the eyes of a boy who can't be much older than me and seen the pain, anger, and disillusionment that he feels. There is definitely a connection made — here I sit with an entire container of cookies and right across from me is this boy in rags holding his hand out.

I am overcome by such a powerful feeling that it brings me to tears. I am probably the most unemotional person you could know. Unfortunately, my experiences have shaped my perception that way. But for this one moment, my rock-hard sheath opens. For the first time, I understand the dire gap between the two worlds I have been exposed to. I not only feel connected to this boy's situation but also somehow feel that I might even be partly responsible for his circumstance.

It was then, at age 12, that I knew something was utterly wrong in the way I had perceived the world to be. It wasn't as prosperous and cheerful as I had always thought. Righteousness did not always prevail. Giving the boy my container of cookies was not enough: I had to do more.

The four months I spent traveling that summer were definitely an experience of a lifetime. Returning to my comfortable lifestyle in Philadelphia was just not going to cut it. My mom has always been quite supportive in developing my ideas of helping others, for she had made it her own life's purpose. She actually handed me the newspaper article that turned my life around.

Iqbal Masih, a 12-year-old boy in Lahore, Pakistan was shot and killed after raising his voice against the evils of child labor. He had escaped from the carpet-making industry, spoken against corporations, and given a voice to those who were suffering. He had given talks all over the world, was presented with the Robert Kennedy Human Rights Award, and was even given a scholarship in the US to attend university here. At age 12 he was dead, shot by the carpet mafia in Pakistan.

I headed to the Beaver College library, and over the course of three months researched and documented every piece of information I could get on child labor. Soon it began to make sense. I not only had to acknowledge my blind responsibility in perpetuating the cycle, but also I had to develop a strategy to unravel it.

So began the formation of Free the Children, in Pennsylvania. We believe in giving a voice to those who can't be heard. We, as students and children, not only have the responsibility but also the obligation to help those who are suffering due to actions we unknowingly make.

After raising awareness in our schools and communities through education, after pressuring our government officials and world leaders to make the education and protection of children a priority, after raising money to build schools and rehabilitation centers in India and elsewhere, I still continue to struggle. We have a long way to go and a rocky road ahead, but I will not be silenced. How can I be? I have a responsibility to project the voices, blood, toil, and tears of 280 million kids from ages 3 to 18 to the people of the Western Hemisphere. It is just my way of undoing a wrong that I had unknowingly committed.

September 26, 2000

I am standing at the Colonial Parking Headquarters, in Washington, DC. I am chanting for the creation of jobs with justice, for equality for the working class, for an end to corporate America. Someone once told to me to speak truth to power. I have taken this advice and run with it. I really do believe we stand in the right.

Over the past six years, I have been able to gain much knowledge about the world in which I live. It really is an ugly picture. After researching the effects of globalization on Third World countries, I

began to realize that human rights violations — child soldiers in Africa's diamond wars; women and child sweatshop workers in Guatemala turning to prostitution; drug rings in South America, the Middle East, and Southeast Asia — and corporate profit-making are inextricably intertwined. Globalization, while it benefits First World countries, has absolutely dire effects in other parts of the world.

We still live in a world full of muck. Many days I wonder if any of my actions cause any impact in the rest of the world. Then I step back and realize that I am only responsible for my actions. Maya Angelou once said, "You may hurt me with your actions, but still, like the dust I'll rise." I must say, it is a hard struggle each day. The most disturbing notion is that people here in America just don't care or are too oblivious to care. Do they not see the children crying for food, the women screaming for help, the men dying for hope? Gandhi once said, "The only thing necessary for the triumph of evil is that good men should do nothing." We might be getting pretty damn close to that.

Still, I do not lose hope. Some call it youthful optimism; I call it vision. If change has to happen, it happens through me. It is not some inevitable force or some coincidence. It is the combined voices of millions working to create change. The notion that I hold most sacred is that we are in the right. Regardless of what the 'Big People' say to justify their actions, regardless of how may lies they tell us, I know that what I'm doing is right.

If I could offer one piece of advice to others who begin to lose hope, it would be to remind them that they are the voice for those who can't be heard. Here, we have so many resources for creating a significant impact. Our voices will be heard and we will not be silenced. We must and will be able to persevere, to see the light. I say opportunity knocks when all hope is lost, and it's our job to prove it. Children in Third World countries, like the boy I met on the train, are not to blame. We need to permanently eradicate the child labor and poverty that mar the face of humankind.

Roli Khare is currently a student at George Washington University, majoring in international politics and economics. She is founder and president of Free the Children, in Pennsylvania, and is involved with the Progressive Students Union, Students for a Free Tibet, and United Students against Sweatshops.

▶ 3.

The Roots of My Resistance

From Rhetoric to Reality

| CHRIS DIXON |

Chris Dixon

On Tuesday, November 30, 1999, I was in downtown Seattle — an unremarkable place amidst remarkable circumstances. Directly in front of me stood a reinforced line of police in full body armor, carrying clubs, rubber bullet guns, and grenade launchers. All around me, hundreds of protesters packed into a solid human wall, taking up half a block. And directly behind us in the middle of an intersection, at least another 100 people surrounded a large wooden platform underpinned by metal pipes. Each pipe had the arm of an activist carefully secured inside. Resolute and defiant, we were there to stay.

"This is the Seattle police," an amplified voice crackled. The rest was drowned out by the booming discharge of a grenade launcher and the foreboding hiss of tear gas, punctuated by the rapid shots of rubber bullets. Suddenly we were scrambling, coughing, gasping, and crying. With shoves and confused stumbling, we fled. Yet just as quickly, we returned, this time with bandanas on our faces and water for our eyes.

Together, we were visibly and physically confronting the logic of global capital — the assumption that multinational corporations somehow have the natural right to move freely, dismantling any barriers that interfere with their profit margin. In short, we were there to shut down the World Trade Organization.

That week in Seattle was the culmination of months of work by countless people. I was one among them. In fact, I was at the midsummer meetings when we launched the Direct Action Network, one of the organizations that put out a call to "shut down the WTO" in Seattle. At the time, those words seemed like an idle wish, an impossible dream. At best, we hoped to be a significant blip on the nightly news and perhaps a noticeable inconvenience to trade delegates. Yet, for the first time in my activist experience, the rhetoric became the reality. On that Tuesday, the first day of WTO Ministerial meetings, most sessions were canceled because we had so successfully blockaded the Convention Center. And by the end of the week, the Ministerial was deadlocked by a coalition of delegates from Asia, Africa, and South America, who stubbornly refused to sign on to an agenda in which they had little voice.

Those heady days were incredibly transformative for me, as I imagine they were for many others. For one, I experienced our collective capacity to make an imprint upon history. Moreover, I saw that 'inevitabilities,' like power, wealth, even capitalist globalization, could be challenged and changed. It was a passionate, intensely liberating moment. And predictably, a week after the Seattle protests, *Newsweek* tried to capture it, announcing "a new mood of radical activism of a kind — and perhaps — scale not seen for years." Other media sources trumpeted this sensationalized surprise at the 'new radicals,' as if we had just plopped down from out of nowhere. Their analysis, vacant as it was, also verged on being willfully ahistorical. I

was no neophyte, nor were most of the young people around me. My presence and commitment in Seattle — like the movements that converged there — grew from deep roots, not fads. My determination was a product of my radicalization.

Activists are made, not born. My story begins in Anchorage, Alaska with a black permanent marker and a secondhand army jacket. At 13, I took the marker and scrawled "I SUPPORT RADICAL DISSIDENCE" on the back of my jacket. The most common response I got was: Is 'Radical Dissidence' a band? Despite the bewilderment and questions from my friends, that message was an important hallmark — a graphic representation of my radicalization.

My true wake-up call came by way of two radicals — a closeted queer man and a Black woman. The man was Tim, my anarchist high school teacher, and the woman was Angela Davis, the undaunted revolutionary, whom I saw speak in Anchorage in 1990. Together, they fundamentally challenged everything that I had ever known. In a word, they embodied dissent. Writer Paul Rogat Loeb, who spent years interviewing students and coming to understand their political choices, encapsulates my experience quite well: "For students who grow up insulated and protected, the stories that stir their souls often come through involvement with foreign worlds." For me, the 'foreign world' was that of dissidents dismantling my comfortable reality, as Tim and Angela so clearly did.

Time has flown since those days. And I've long since retired my tattered army jacket, though not its spirit. In the process, I've found a vibrant sense of hope. I saw the first sparkles as a teenager, in the small-scale efforts of my friends and I as we asked hard questions and struggled for democratic control over our school. They shone brighter as I discovered courageous groups of people steadfastly organizing against poverty, imprisonment, corporate-sponsored environmental devastation, police brutality, institution-alized racism and sexism, labor exploitation, and the many other faces of systemic injustice. That everyday resistance is still what keeps me afloat.

I've found additional hope in learning to confront my privilege. Little did I know at age 13 that serious radical dissidence also means critically understanding the social forces that have shaped me as a white, middle-class, seemingly straight guy in a society founded upon structural inequalities. And I still have much to learn. Patriarchy, white supremacy, capitalism, heterosexism, and other systems of oppression have awarded me considerable privilege and comfort, blinding and cutting me off from the daily realities of most people. Consequently, dissidence — directed both outward and inward — has offered an important tool for challenging and changing not only the world, but also myself.

Confronting privilege is hardly an individual project. In fact, the hope that I've found here largely comes from understanding my small efforts as part of broader radical currents crossing and critically addressing race, class, gender, and sexuality, among others. All together, they hold the vital promise of building, in the words of organizer Helen Luu, "a movement (or movements) that is dedicated to bringing down all forms of oppression simultaneously with challenging global capitalism."

Privileged folks like me have a lot to learn from those who experience the brunt of marginalization and oppression. People of color, working class folks, women, indigenous peoples, queers,

immigrants, and many others have been engaged in inspiring, frequently interconnected, struggles for a long, long time. I find hope, then, as I continue to learn how to work as an authentic ally. It's necessarily a difficult, protracted process but always enriching.

I've also located hope in the wisdom of elder radicals such as Peter Bohmer. His striking emphasis is that everyone can contribute to social change in both small and large ways. Seemingly small efforts can have important — and far-reaching — results. Educating others creatively, establishing community and cultural centers, demanding authentic public oversight of police, building art installations, organizing in our workplaces, sustaining nurturing relationships, constructing alternative media, struggling for control over our schools, painting graffiti, planting community gardens, protesting welfare cuts, confronting oppression in our daily lives — these and many more contributions can be immeasurably powerful and deeply inspiring. Seen as complementary demands and tactics, these actions harbor valuable lessons about challenging power, fermenting social change, and developing directly democratic control over our lives. Indeed, they are the potential building blocks of vivacious, diverse movements capable of making key gains and ultimately transforming our society. It is an approach that resonates for me.

Though I've seen the astounding success of large, more militant actions, in my experience, the scale of activism doesn't always correspond with its potential impact. I think, in particular, of the widespread success of a handful of us graduating students at The Evergreen State College in 1999. We stubbornly organized to have political prisoner Mumia Abu-Jamal as a commencement speaker. Our small efforts created a more animated public discussion of Mumia's case and of the US criminal (in)justice system than did the 35,000 people who had marched in support of him just two months earlier. With some ingenuity, luck, and determination, we discovered that we could make a substantial contribution.

I caught another glimmer of hope in 1997 — long before most anyone had even heard of the WTO. Some other Americans and I joined young Canadian radicals in Vancouver who were organizing to "crash the summit" of the Asia-Pacific Economic Cooperation (APEC) — a free trade agreement between a number of Asian economies, Canada, and the US.

Those radicals unabashedly took their inspiration from people in the global South, like those who protested the preceding APEC summit in the Philippines and faced severe state repression; and from indigenous peoples worldwide who have resisted a colonial project spanning centuries. The Vancouver activists consciously saw their actions as part of a rich history of international anti-capitalist struggle. And when they went to disrupt the

summit, they were met with a level of police violence that clearly anticipated what we would later see at the WTO protests. Two years later, on the streets of Seattle, I took my inspiration from those Canadians and the tradition of resistance in which they so determinedly embedded themselves.

For me, shutting down the WTO was at once a continuation and a beginning — rooted in a personal and historical legacy of struggle and hope, yet harboring a new potential for collective action.

I remember it best as a single moment on November 30 when everything paused. A radical dance troupe performed wordlessly in an occupied intersection as hundreds hummed "Amazing Grace" (an echo of an earlier movement). This was the same pregnant pause I recall noticing as Mumia's prerecorded speech played during my college graduation. Indeed, this was the very same pause that I remember feeling at 13 when I heard Angela Davis shout, "Fight the power!" Those magical moments are hints of hope woven into an artful tapestry of struggle. They've sustained me since my earliest days of marker pen and army jacket.

I actually haven't changed all that much over the years. I'm still a firmly rooted radical punk rock kid from Alaska. I still grapple with the privileges that have been afforded me. And I'm still relentlessly hopeful. These days I'm particularly excited because so many promising organizing efforts are afoot across the world. Movements are growing, innovative actions are multiplying, we're learning from each other, and élites are increasingly defensive. For sure, radical change isn't just around the corner. We seem, however, to be in the midst of an upsurge. The old adage, 'The sixties are over,' is disappearing as we build a resistance that, while owing a debt to the old, also transcends it.

In April of 2000, shortly after the Washington, DC protests against the World Bank and the International Monetary Fund, *Time* weighed in with an article entitled "The New Radicals." "Are they dreamers," the subtitle asked pointedly, "or sly subversives?" At first glance, it looks as though either way — as starry-eyed idealists or conniving troublemakers — us young radicals are easily dismissed. But taken another way, what about both? To dream is to imagine a different world, and to be slyly subversive is to start by strategically revolutionizing this one. In that light, with our respective roots and some hope, I'd say that *Time* might be on to something. The point now is to insure that the tradition of dreams and subversion continues. It didn't start in Seattle and it won't end in Qatar. Collectively, across the globe, we'll have to make sure that it doesn't.

▼

Chris Dixon is a radical Alaskan activist, and writer. He is presently working on a book, Critical Hope *and is organizing with a loose network of folks trying to build broader-based movements.*

▶ 4.

The Global Rule Makers
Undermining Democracy Around the World

| GLOBAL EXCHANGE AND PUBLIC CITIZEN |

NEVA WELTON

The WTO was established in 1995 during the GATT (General Agreement on Tariffs and Trade) Uruguay Round Agreements. Created to expand and enforce GATT, the World Trade Organization is the most powerful legislative and judicial body in the world. The expansion of GATT and the establishment of the WTO were proclaimed as a means of enhancing the creation of global wealth and prosperity and promoting the well-being of all people in all member states.

In reality, the WTO and GATT Uruguay Round Agreements have functioned principally to pry open markets for the benefit of transnational corporations at the expense of national and local economies; workers, farmers, indigenous peoples, women, and other social groups; health and safety; the environment; and animal welfare. In the years of its existence, WTO panels composed of corporate attorneys have consistently ruled in favor of multinational corporations.

By promoting the free trade agenda of multinational corporations under rules and procedures that are undemocratic, non-transparent, and non-accountable, the WTO has systematically undermined democracy around the world. According to the WTO, our democratically elected public officials no longer have the rights to protect the environment and public health. WTO rules and rulings can be enforced through sanctions, which gives the WTO more power than any other international body and even national governments.

WORLD BANK/INTERNATIONAL MONETARY FUND

Created after World War II to help avoid Great Depression-like economic disasters, the World Bank and the IMF are the world's largest public lenders, with the Bank managing a total portfolio of $200 billion and the Fund supplying member governments with money to overcome short-term credit crunches.

The World Bank and the IMF are accused of being the world's biggest loan sharks, and for good reason. When the Bank and the Fund lend money to debtor countries, the money comes with strings attached. These strings come in the form of policy prescriptions called 'structural adjustment policies' (SAPs). SAPs require debtor governments to open their economies to penetration by foreign corporations, which allows access to the country's workers and environment at bargain basement prices.

Structural adjustment policies mean the across-the-board privatization of public utilities and publicly owned industries. They mean the slashing of government budgets, which leads to cutbacks in spending on health care and education. They mean focusing resources on growing export crops for industrial countries rather than on supporting family farms and growing food for local communities. And, as their imposition in country after country in

Latin America, Africa, and Asia has shown, they lead to deeper inequality and environmental destruction.

For decades, people in the Third World have protested the way the World Bank and IMF undemocratically impose such policies on their countries. Beginning in 1999, those protests have spread to the power centers of the developed world. In April 2000, some 20,000 people gathered in Washington, DC during the institutions' spring meetings to demand a more democratic, international decision-making process. Similar protests took place later that year in Prague, Czech Republic and another was planned in Washington, DC in September 2001. By dragging the Bank and the Fund into the light of public scrutiny, these protests have re-invigorated a public dialogue about the growing wealth inequalities within and among nations, and have put the institutions on notice that they can't continue business as usual.

NORTH AMERICAN FREE TRADE AGREEMENT

NAFTA is the trade agreement between the governments of Canada, the United Mexican States, and the United States of America. The objectives of NAFTA, as stated in the formal agreement are to:

(a) eliminate barriers to trade in, and facilitate the cross-border movement of, goods and services between the territories of the Parties;

(b) promote conditions of fair competition in the free trade area;

(c) increase substantially investment opportunities in their territories;

(d) provide adequate and effective protection and enforcement of intellectual property rights in each Party's territory;

(e) create effective procedures for the implementation and application of this Agreement, and for its joint administration and the resolution of disputes; and

(f) establish a framework for further trilateral, regional, and multilateral cooperation to expand and enhance the benefits of this Agreement.

A quick look at NAFTA's legacy reveals disastrous consequences:

- It's estimated that over a million US jobs have been lost since NAFTA, as companies relocated to Mexico to take advantage of the weaker labor standards. These workers usually find jobs with less security and wages that are about 77 percent of what they originally had.

- The US trade surplus with Mexico has become an $18.6 billion deficit.

- Despite promises of increased economic development throughout Mexico, only the border region has seen intensified industrial activity. Yet even this small gain has not brought prosperity. Over one million more Mexicans work for less than the minimum wage of $3.40 per day today than before NAFTA, and during the NAFTA period, eight million Mexicans have fallen from the middle class into poverty.

- In addition, the increase of border industry has created worsening environmental and public health threats in the area. Along the border, the occurrence of some diseases, including hepatitis, is two or three times the national average, due to lack of sewage treatment and safe drinking water.

FREE TRADE AREA OF THE AMERICAS (FTAA)

FTAA is the formal name given to an expansion of NAFTA (the North American Free Trade Agreement) that would include nearly all of the countries in the Western Hemisphere and is to be implemented no later than 2005. This massive expansion is currently being negotiated in secret by trade ministers from a total of 34 nations in North, Central, and South America, and the Caribbean. The goal of the FTAA is to impose the NAFTA model of increased privatization and deregulation across the hemisphere.

Imposition of the FTAA would empower corporations to constrain governments from setting standards for public health and safety, safeguarding their workers, and ensuring that corporations do not pollute the communities in which they operate. Effectively, these rules would handcuff governments' public interest policymaking and enhance corporate control at the expense of citizens throughout the Americas.

▶ 5.

Globalization
An Unprecedented Assault Against Human Values

| NOAM CHOMSKY |

FROM AN EMAIL DATED 6/21/00 4:01:46 PM, CHOMSKY@MIT.EDU WRITES:

You asked me what I think are the major issues right now. I think, with many ramifications, the major issues have to do with what is misleadingly called 'globalization,' which is actually a highly specific form of socioeconomic planning and international integration geared to the interests of unaccountable private power — tyrannies, in fact, called 'corporations.' The interests of others are, at best, incidental.

One consequence of this is that for about three-quarters of the US workforce, incomes have stagnated or declined for the past 20 years, while working hours have increased enormously, to the highest in the industrial world. Another is that social indicators — what really counts in measuring quality of life — have declined steadily for 25 years after increasing steadily, along with the growth of the economy, before that. There are similar consequences elsewhere, worse in the poor countries.

Meanwhile, economic growth has also declined significantly, but none of this matters to those running the show or their cheerleaders, because the small segment of the global population to

DONNA COVENEY

▲

Noam Chomsky

| 25 |

which they belong is doing fine. A crucial feature of all of this is a major assault against democracy. This takes several forms. One is financial liberalization, which undercuts popular sovereignty by providing concentrated private capital with a kind of veto power over government decisions: if they are 'irrational' (meaning, only helping people, not profits), then the government can be punished by capital flight, attack on the currency, etc. That's highly effective.

The trade agreements, too, are designed to transfer the decision making to private power and the international bureaucracies constructed to work for them (IMF, World Trade Organization, etc.). They are also designed to make labor markets more 'flexible,' which is a fancy way of saying that when you go to sleep at night, you don't know whether you have a job tomorrow, or what kind of a job. That leads to 'worker insecurity,' which is hailed as a great boon to the economy, because working people are too intimidated to seek wage increases and benefits. Also, threat of job transfer across the border, for example, has proven to be an effective device to hamper union organizing (illegally, but that doesn't matter when the government doesn't enforce the laws).

To induce people to submit to all of this, there has been a huge and unprecedented assault against elementary human values, in an attempt to bring people to see themselves as nothing more than atoms of meaningless consumption; all very carefully designed, and for good reasons. Schools have to be 'corporatized,' designed to turn out interchangeable cogs who are obedient, passive, and narrow-minded — except for the rich and privileged sector, for whom resources (including educational resources) are concentrated. The schools

ANOTHER VOICE

Many talk about the inevitability of globalization, meaning only corporate globalization. But there is another kind of globalization going on, and it will be much harder to stop: the globalization of activism, on the Internet and on the streets, and the globalization of feeling.
— Peter Kirn

must be 'institutions for the indoctrination of the young,' as liberal élites describe them when they are writing for one another — not expecting outsiders to read it.

What does this mean for young people? This is the world they're inheriting, and it is an ugly and dangerous one. To the limited extent that market systems function (much more limited than is recognized), they 'underprice' public goods — like the environment, for example; that means the legacy of future generations. That could be extremely serious not far down the road. They also 'underprice' collective risk, like the risk of nuclear war, severe and growing. That's not to speak of the deleterious economic, social, cultural, and moral effect of these forms of domination and repression. This only scratches the surface.

There's more than enough here to keep plenty of activists busy for a long, long time; and probably not too much time to deal with it. You asked if I have hope? Sure, there's always hope, and history shows that over time a lot of it is justified. But it's never been an easy path and never will be.

Noam Chomsky, the man Bono dubbed 'the rebel with a cause,' lives in Boston, where he teaches linguistics at MIT. An outspoken anarchist and libertarian socialist, for the past 60 years he has devoted himself to questioning the media and its relationship to governments and the corporate élite.

▶ 6.

Changing Culture
Choosing Life over Money

| KEVIN DANAHER |

Kevin Danaher

I do a lot of speaking on college campuses and what I say to students is: You are far more sophisticated that we ever were as a movement. The motivation of our movement, the anti-Vietnam War movement, was fear. We didn't want to go to a far-off land and kill people or be killed.

The movement of young people today is far different. There is an element of fear, of course, because they see their planet being destroyed; they see the biosphere's basic systems breaking down. So, understandably they are concerned. I try to encourage them in their concern but not in an apocalyptic direction.

The question is: How bad does it have to get before people wake up? How many canaries have to die in the coal mine before even the dumbest miner, even the Rush Limbaugh ditto-heads say: Aw gee, something's going on here; we better get active before it all comes apart. The truth is, people my age (in their 50s) are going to be dead before the doo-doo really hits the fan.

I think it's easy to predict the way things are going to happen. The environmental crisis is going to exhibit undeniable, severe symptoms as the years go by and the social crisis will similarly exacerbate.

Even now, an increasing number of young people are seeing that there's a social crisis — thousands of children are dying from hunger. Children are dying from measles, when a vaccine costs ten cents. They see the inequality growing. Even the World Bank and other ruling institutions admit that the inequality is growing.

Then, you have an environmental crisis that is threatening things (like the ozone layer) upon which we all depend for our existence. The polar ice caps are melting. The glaciers are in retreat. We have topsoil loss at an unsustainable rate and ground water pollution, all signs of systemic breakdown that can't be ignored.

Those crises are in turn creating a third crisis, which I would label a spiritual crisis. You have millions of people here in the affluent part of the planet who turn their heads. They see the house on fire; they see the child screaming from the upstairs window, and they say: I've got to go to the library and read a book about combustion because I don't know enough about fires. They cop out.

That moral bankruptcy must be addressed. The question is: How do you reach the public mind? How do you reach the public heart and spirit? To say: Look, there's an emergency; there's a crisis and you want to go out to the mall instead of going to vote?

There's a crisis of powerlessness. People are walking around saying: I'm only one person. What can I do? I can't fight city hall. If there's a revolution, then the new leadership will be just as bad as the old. Well, if that were true, then there'd still be slavery. Women wouldn't have the right to vote. We wouldn't have civil rights legislation. We wouldn't have the 40-hour workweek.

People don't realize that workers in China don't have the weekend. We do because we fought and people actually died to get the 40-hour week. In China where Nike, Hewlett-Packard, Levi-Strauss, and other companies make their products to sell us, people don't have the weekend. They don't have the right to form trade unions; they don't have the right to speak freely or worship as they choose. Yet US companies are happy to go there and make money.

What's great about the youth movement is that youth see this kind of hypocrisy and moral bankruptcy, and they're willing to go out in the street and protest. In fact, the youth movement has succeeded in changing the very nature of the culture. If you look at the way these protests are organized at the WTO meetings in Seattle or in Washington, DC, there are no generals. It's all lieutenants. It's a very flat hierarchy. It's more like a hub and spokes.

Each affinity group is organized in small groups. It's very open, very participatory. Everybody gets the right to speak. It's a real democratic culture. Not democracy like every few years you go into a booth and punch holes in a piece of cardboard. But a truly democratic process where it's participatory and not 'representative.' To me, this is very encouraging.

In my pubic education work, I encourage young people. I say: Go for it. You're on the right track. And I'm totally encouraged by the power, the vitality, and the diversity of this movement and the willingness to be self-critical.

Even before the Seattle protest ended, people were saying: Well, you know, there should have been more people of color here. What did we do wrong in our organizing that it wasn't more diverse? And it was pretty damn diverse. It was more diverse than the people who run this country — the corporations, the World Bank, the IMF, the WTO. And yet the movement was very self-critical.

The key tactic that we have, that the élite will never have, is mass mobilizing. We can mass mobilize the citizenry. They, by their very definition as an élite ruling class, do not do that and will not do that. They are more into mass demobilizing. They want people to go to the Super Bowl or World Series or to watch TV. They don't want people to go out en masse into the streets to protest for change.

If we can perfect the art and science of how to democratically mass mobilize, we can force just about any policy change. You name a policy — transportation, housing, energy, food — you give me 10,000 people in the streets and we'll change that policy, because they can't ignore thousands of people in the street. They can tear gas us, trash us in the press, but that shows their weakness, not their strength. If they were really strong, they would debate us in public arenas and win the debate in the public mind. They know they can't, so they shun debate.

At Global Exchange, we're focused on the central issue of corporate power. The corporations have not only taken over the economy, our food, our transportation, energy, things of that sort; they've also taken over our government. The youth movement sees this, knows it's wrong, and has developed a critique of corporate power. They're willing to go out and confront corporate power in all of its manifestations.

FORREST LARWAIN-HAWES

▲

Seattle WTO protest

More and more youth are grasping that there are two basic worldviews out there: the money cycle and the life cycle. Under the money value system, a 2,000-year-old redwood is not a gift of the creator; it's $300,000 worth of lumber. That ideology will destroy nature.

I think the movement is at a critical point now. All of the different pieces of the movement — like the anti-sweatshop

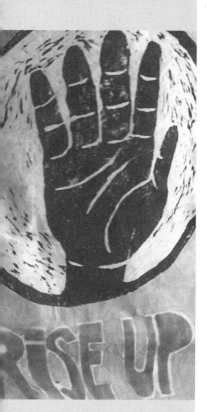

▲

Art & Revolution banner

Kevin Danaher is the cofounder of Global Exchange in San Francisco and has written and edited many books dealing with US foreign policy, including Globalize This! The Battle against the World Trade Organization and Corporate Rule.

movement, save the trees, biotechnology — are starting to realize: Look, we're each fingers and we've got to come together as a fist. Their starting question is how to build unity within the movement. And as long as people keep asking that question, we will develop an organizational response.

One of the tricky skills to develop is to take the anger and the pain and transform it into positive energy. In those dark moments of the soul, you have to say: Do I really have a right to wallow in self-despair because maybe we won't succeed? Or do you have an obligation to little kids dying in Africa or somewhere else, and have to say: Come on, let's get back in the ring. You've had your few moments of wallowing; now let's go out and kick some corporate ass!

The social change movement is not a destination you reach and then relax, but a mode of travel – a way of life. I'm thankful every morning when I wake up that I know what my life is about. And it came out of a negative experience of seeing suffering and injustice that we in this country can only imagine the depths of. There's a way to make that experience positive, and it has me fired up to be self-directed toward a goal where all of our children can enjoy a decent school and all of our children have enough to eat. That's part of what this struggle is all about. It's redefining that personal pronoun 'our,' as in the expression 'children on the face of the Earth are our children.' We must get people to feel that, really deeply, and act on it. If we can do that, we can change every problem that's out there.

▶ 7.

Art and Revolution
Revitalizing Political Protest

| ALLI STARR |

The role of the revolutionary artist is to make revolution irresistible.
— *Toni Cade Bambara*

I come from a long line of outspoken women. For years, my mother worked on political campaigns within the system, experiencing one defeat after another. Eventually, she came to value nonviolent direct action tactics and civil disobedience; in the early '80s, she joined thousands of others in the antinuclear movement. As the police dragged her away, she would point to a photo of my sister and me that she wore pinned to her shirt to explain why she needed to be there. Our corporate-controlled media would have us believe such actions are futile, but anti-nuke campaigns successfully educated millions of people about the dangers of radioactive energy. And the proliferation of nuclear power plants was halted. My mother's courage has been a powerful inspiration for me.

To be awake to the necessity for activism is to become aware that our very survival and the survival of life on Earth are in great peril. Indigenous cultures world-wide are being annihilated; more than two million poor and working class people are living in prisons in the US; communities of color are targeted for toxic waste sites. It is crucial that we recognize which communities are negatively impacted for the benefit of others. We need to find innovative ways to

▲

Alli Starr

challenge a system that puts profit before people, and we need to create ways to welcome new people into a compassionate movement for social and environmental justice. This became clear in my own life when, after working for years as a professional dancer, I began to feel that the dance world was not responding to the needs of the community.

I wanted to see artists think beyond their personal goals and wake up to the fact that people all over the world were suffering from the effects of our relative comfort. In 1995, my friend David Solnit (a carpenter with a direct action background) and I started working together. David was looking for ways to revitalize political protest; I was interested in bringing more creativity and creative people into social justice movements. The fusion of our visions and talents ultimately birthed Art and Revolution.

DAVID HANKS

DC IMF protest

For seven months, David and I traveled across the country, from San Francisco to Philadelphia, bringing giant puppets to a Boston housing action, challenging Detroit's Fermi II nuclear power plant, and demonstrating in support of political prisoner Mumia Abu-Jamal. During the Democratic National Convention in Chicago in 1996, we helped plan a street festival as part of Active Resistance — a conference of more than 700 activists. We built a 20-foot-tall (6-meter-tall) headless 'tower-man' adorned with corporate logos and carrying puppets — representing presidential candidates — in his giant hands. He was pulled along by 'straining' people representing voters, taxpayers, and workers. Effigies of tree stumps, single mothers, and body bags — representing education, welfare, and healthcare — dragged along behind him. People from the neighborhood, intrigued by the theater, came out of their houses and businesses to watch. Art has a way of touching hearts and minds in a way no speech or flier can.

In 1997, we produced the first Art and Revolution convergence, offering three days of dance, theater, music, and puppet-making workshops. We also taught media, anti-racism, and nonviolent direct action skills to the 200 people who came from all over the country. On the fourth day, we held a festival of resistance on the streets of Seattle.

The overwhelming coverage we receive suggests that even mainstream media are captivated by art with a message. Reporters often ask if puppets and performers will be at upcoming demonstrations. However, because art is so effective at reaching people, the police have increased their attacks on our puppets and props. In 1996, on the last day of our Chicago counter-convention, police without nametags or numbers raided our puppet space, using pepper spray indiscriminately. Later, they denied everything, even after two people were reported to have been hospitalized due to the effects of pepper spray. In Los Angeles, during the Democratic National Convention in 2000, the police tried to steal our "Goddess of Democracy" puppet, but the people prevailed and won her back.

ANOTHER **VOICE**

Creative activism is about building a new way, rather than simply demolishing the old. By doing this we create a firm foundation for sustainable, community-centered government and a strong belief system to replace the empty promises of religion, technology, and consumerism. If we are asking people to abandon these beliefs, we must at least be offering them something better.

— Faith Thomas

Collaborative creativity, the antithesis of war, is inherently positive and disarming. Almost nowhere was this more apparent than in Seattle, where more than 50,000 activists shut down the first day of the 1999 World Trade Organization meeting. Dance, music, and giant images helped to hold blockades, de-escalate police violence, and create a joyful festival for global justice. One powerful example of this occurred as thousands of people filled the intersection in front of the Sheraton Hotel. The police were clad in Darth Vader-like riot gear, and the atmosphere was thick with tension. Yet, through the tear gas, six women dressed all in black began to dance in slow-motion unison on top of a platform, where dozens of youth activists were locked down. Hundreds sang together — in rich harmony. In a moment of transcendence, the sun, which had been obscured by rain and clouds, emerged, and the police violence stopped almost immediately. At that instant, as in many throughout the day, we activists stood unified and strong.

Art and Revolution is a collective of artists and activists who revitalize political protest by bridging creative culture with struggles for social justice. We have continued as a Bay Area-based collective but have grown to include dance activists Danza Sin Fronteras and the *a cappella* group Harmonic Intervention, as well as several sister Art and Revolution collectives that thrive throughout the country. We bring dance, music, theater, and giant puppets to the streets to bring attention to the crucial issues of our times. Acknowledging that our struggles are inherently interconnected, we are committed to working in solidarity and sharing art activism skills with diverse communities and to empowering allies to create theater that addresses their community's issues.

Although contemporary Western culture divides creative work and social responsibility, political street theater has long enjoyed an honorable history all over the world. We are honored to follow in the footsteps of thousands who have contributed to this lineage. Our work has been most deeply inspired by Augusto Boal of Brazil, Butoh dancers of Japan, the Bread and Puppet Theater of Vermont, the San Francisco Mime Troupe, Contra-band, and Wise Fool Puppet Intervention of San Francisco.

I believe that our political organizing suffers without creative vision in the same way that our art making suffers without social, political, and/or community relevance. If we are to survive, we must wed our creative voices with our strategies for positive change. We have a historic opportunity to launch a widespread movement based on the power of mutual respect, egalitarian decision making, and creativity. It is time we created a global web of creative resistance against corporate domination. Through cultural intervention, we reclaim our humanity and enact our liberation. Let the art revolution begin!

Alli Starr is the cofounder of Art and Revolution and the annual Reclaim May Day festival. She is the founder of Cultural Links, which houses several socially conscious arts projects, including: Art in Action, youth empowerment summer camps, the Radical Performance Fest, Danza Sin Fronteras, and the Power to the People Road Shows.

LINKS

www.artandrevolution.org

▶ 8.

Joy and Justice
Stone Soup Cooperative

| JEFF PINZINO |

▼

Jeff Pinzino
(standing far right)

MEHRDAD AZEMUN

The sign over the doorway in the living room of Stone Soup Cooperative reads, "Don't Postpone Joy." The couches are packed with 30 activists who have just rolled up in a 1960s-era city bus on their way from the Bay Area to DC. Our home is an oasis along the road to the IMF/World Bank demonstrations, where these 30 will join thousands of others, including a dozen Stone Soup members in protesting the destructive tendencies of the global economy. The conversation is lively, ranging from testimonials of the recent protests in Seattle to questions about co-op living to an exchange of recipes for vegan brownies. We feast together on homemade bean soup and fresh cornbread. Many of the travelers take the opportunity to go upstairs and grab a much-needed shower. After dinner, our visitors meet to decide their immediate plans. Unwittingly, we find ourselves responsible for their hardest decision to date — several people are so excited by the co-op that they don't want to leave.

Stone Soup has been my home and inspiration for the last four years. I'm a 28-year-old Chicago community organizer and one of 18 permanent residents of a building that was a convent before it was an activist co-op. I feel honored to live in a place that has always been a home for those called to live out their conscience in the modern world. I came to Stone Soup through a series of potluck dinners that took place in a friend's living room across town. There, I found other organizers, teachers, artists, and community workers who understood the passion and frustration that I was feeling and that is typical of many people doing work for social justice. I also found delicious food and conversation, music and laughter. When someone brought up the idea of finding a space to live where we could have this kind of sharing all the time, I jumped at the chance. I remember how easily the name came to us. It is based on a children's story of a village of people who individually were starving but collectively had enough food to feed everybody. We continue our tradition of feeding each other at potlucks every Tuesday night.

"Joy and Justice" has become our mission, our motto, and our mantra. We believe that joy without justice is hollow, and justice without joy is boring. Joy and Justice invoke the spirit of love and possibility encapsulated in any true work for social change. It is an antidote for the alienation and apathy that is commonly found today, even among those people working to heal the world.

Often, our living room feels like the staging area for a revolution. It may be stacked with sleeping gear and duffle bags for a busload of people going to the School of the Americas demonstration in Georgia, 10-foot puppets on their way to an affordable housing

march in the neighborhood, or trays of food ready for a Food Not Bombs action on the streets of Chicago. It's also the traditional debriefing room for those returning from the front. You might hear an eyewitness account of Iraqi children dying in their mothers' arms for want of a $2 medicine. An election monitor from East Timor might share her experience of being unable to leave a school building because of gunfire outside. You might hear a description of the chaos and creativity of volunteers racing to keep up with the protests from inside the Independent Media Center at the 2000 Democratic National Convention. At Stone Soup, we have a unique window on the world of social justice in the 21st century.

We embody Emma Goldman's declaration, "If I can't dance, it's not my revolution." We strive to be as sophisticated in our work for joy as in our work for justice. Recently, our living room was the site of the Venetian Pancake Festival, coinciding with a visit by clown doctor and humanitarian Patch Adams, and including a triathlon of pancake-inspired Olympic events. We hosted a storytelling circle for fourth graders from a local Montessori School, featuring traditional tales told by a Nigerian political exile staying with us at the time (we later learned the kids had convinced their parents to join in a boycott of Shell Oil). We've also made a commitment to celebrate birthdays in grand style, and the house will do what it can to grant any member's birthday wish. These have ranged from "having the Beatles play at my party" to "finding the meaning of life." One request to "live the great poem" was met with a full-scale re-enactment of Dante's *Divine Comedy* — a tour through co-op inferno, purgatory, and paradise.

Stone Soup is a model of the kind of world I'm struggling for. We relate to each other from a deep sense of love and nonviolence. When there is conflict, there's an understanding that we need to come to a resolution that we can all live with. All our meetings are consensus-based, so when any decision is made, everyone's needs must be considered. There is a high level of trust for all involved. Fun is a priority, and Stone Soup is a playful, often silly environment. When I'm here I laugh a lot, think a lot, learn a lot, and am almost never lonely. After a frustrating day of organizing in the neighborhood where I work, I can come home to a reminder of why it's all worth doing.

Our traveling protesters are just a few of the hundreds of visitors that cross our threshold every year. We strive to share the experience of Joy and Justice with each guest that comes through, and often we get back more than we expect. Recently we hosted a Russian writer and his family who are producing a book about community organizing in America. Igor is a trailblazer in his own country, having brought the tools of community development to Russian citizens after the fall of communism destroyed their social safety net. His comments reflect our own hope: "You folks are building a future for America, a true democracy, and I love this America."

Jeff Pinzino is a founding member of Stone Soup Cooperative in Chicago. He has been a community organizer in Chicago for six years, most recently with the Northwest Neighborhood Federation. He is also an action associate for the Interfaith Youth Corps in Chicago.

▶ 9.

Ruckus Society
Training Activists in Nonviolent Direct Action

| JOHN SELLERS |

John Sellers

The Ruckus Society is an interesting community of activists, a unique critter out there in the world of nongovernmental organizations, because we don't have specific campaigns that we work on. We're much more of a support organization. We do our best work and are most rewarded by being of service to different movements in environmental and human rights struggles, fair trade, and labor issues.

Our specialty is the use of nonviolent direct action and civil disobedience. Nonviolent direct action is any kind of action that people take to intervene with a perceived injustice. It could be something as simple as signing a petition or writing a letter or something as profound as hanging off a bridge to stop a nuclear aircraft carrier from coming into port. Civil disobedience is the conscious disobeying of unjust laws. Lots of people confuse those terms or use them interchangeably.

The centerpiece of Ruckus Society is a program we call Action Camp, a four- to six-day dynamic learning experience. We camp out in either a beautiful wilderness area or in the fringes around cities, with anywhere from 100 to 200 people. We teach theoretical workshops in skill areas such as basic training in nonviolent direct action, the use of nonviolence, the history and strategic use of confrontational nonviolence, media for direct action, campaign strategies, direct action planning, scouting and reconnaissance, communications, and political theater. We also spend half our time in physical, hands-on training, teaching technical tree climbing, blockading, and — something we are most well known for — our urban climbing techniques. We also do a lot of role plays to try to bring as much realism in to camp as possible, so folks get an initial perception of what an action is going to be like in the real world.

Action camp is an extremely dynamic and inspiring community. People of all ages come together to share responsibility, take care of one another, share skills and gifts, and gently push each other to do their best work. We get a lot of youth to these camps, and I think they're some of the most dynamic, energetic participants we get. Many of the skills that we share at camp can be directly applied to campaigns being led by young people. Whether they're interested in the environment, social justice, or fair trade, oftentimes you see youth making the connections about globalization more powerfully than anyone because it's just so natural to them.

The Ruckus Society started out as a forest-specific organization, and we really didn't come out of the woods until 1998, when we did our first Human Rights Action Camp. Since that time, we have reached out to and been approached by so many different movements and diverse communities. It's really been an amazing growth process for us and has opened our perception of who we can be.

Part of the growth process has been the general recognition that until the movement accurately reflects the diversity of the greater

Lily Wang – Ruckus Society Action Camp

"THE WORLD SHRINKS OR EXPANDS IN PROPORTION TO ONE'S COURAGE"
-ANAÏS NIN

John Sellers is director of The Ruckus Society. In the 1990s, he sailed with Greenpeace and has traveled extensively throughout North America, coordinating direct actions for Rainforest Action Network, Earth First!, Project Underground, International Campaign for Tibet, Global Exchange, and many others.

LINKS

www.ruckus.org

society in which it exists, it's not going to be a successful movement. In fact, it may even be dishonest to call it a movement — a real movement — until it cuts across the race, gender, and class boundaries that have traditionally been divisive.

At Ruckus, we paid special attention to those concerns when we planned our Action Camps in the summer of 2000 for the Republican and Democratic National Conventions. We partnered up with some incredible social justice organizations and youth organizations of color to bring in very experienced trainers and facilitators. We took our time constructing the camp, because we knew some really deep issues would come up by bringing such diverse communities together. Some really historic lines of privilege and racism, suppression and repression surfaced. Fortunately, we had some amazing people with a lot of patience and love to help the white people. It's not easy to deal with the institutional and personal racism that we have as white people in a society that's been constructed for our benefit to the exclusion of other people. It was an incredible learning experience, and in fact I think many people took away more from that camp than from any other Ruckus Camp.

In the ten years that I've been doing this work professionally, I've never felt better than I do right now. I think that the tide is turning. We're beginning to win. Certainly we're still seeing the loss of habitat and ecosystems and the continued suppression of people in marginalized communities around the planet. On a purely materialistic level, everything that we value is fading fast. It would be easy to get demoralized. But instead we're getting organized, and anyone with their ear to the ground can hear the not so distant thunder of our movement.

▶ 10.

Organizing a New Generation of Activists

The Nuts and Bolts of Working Together

| UNANIMOUS CONSENSUS |

AFFINITY GROUPS (AG)

Affinity groups rose out of the anarchist and workers movement of the late 19th century, during their struggle against fascism in Spain during the Spanish Civil War. In the US, the strategy came back to life in April of 1977, when 2,500 people organized into affinity groups and occupied the Seabrook, New Hampshire nuclear power plant. Since then, it has been used in many successful actions throughout the late 1970s and 1980s, including the Central American solidarity movement, lesbian/gay liberation movement, Earth First!, the Earth liberation movement, and many others.

Affinity groups are self-sufficient, autonomous teams of 5 to

Lockdown
– WTO protest, Seattle

| 45 |

Upper: David Guizar
— Community Self
Determination Institute
Lower: Sommer Garza

20 people who share certain principles, goals, interests, and/or plans that enable them to work together well. Through a decentralized, highly democratic, and powerful process, affinity groups develop and carry out actions alone or collectively as part of a mass action. When acting with other affinity groups, one spokesperson is chosen to represent the group at a spokescouncil meeting.

Affinity groups are vital to any mass nonviolent action for providing support and solidarity to their members. When an affinity group works and acts together, familiarity and trust develop, and feelings of isolation or alienation from the movement or the world in general can be alleviated. By generating familiarity, the affinity group structure also reduces the possibility of infiltration by outside provocateurs.

Affinity groups for mass actions are often formed during nonviolence training sessions. Some affinity groups may only be together for one action, but many stay together and work on other actions, becoming a source of ongoing support. Affinity groups generally operate on a consensus decision-making model.

ROLES WITHIN THE AFFINITY GROUP

Roles should be rotated to share skills, information, and influence.

- **Medical:** You may want to have a trained street medic to deal with any medical or health issues during an action.
- **Legal Observer:** If legal observers are not already in place, then people not involved in the action may want to take notes on police conduct and possible violations of activists' rights.
- **Media:** If you are doing an action that plans to draw media attention, empower a member to act as a spokesperson.

- **Action Elf/Vibes-Watcher:** An Action Elf helps out with the general wellness of the group, supplying water, massages, and encouragement (song or cheers). This role is not essential but may be particularly helpful in daylong actions in which people might become tired or irritable.
- **Traffic:** If your group is on the move, you may need to designate some members to control traffic (stop cars at intersections) and generally watch out for the safety of people on the streets.
- **Arrest-able Members:** Depending on what kind of direct action you are doing, you may require a certain number of members who are willing to be arrested. Or some parts of an action may need a minimum number of arrest-ables. Either way, it is important to know who is doing the action and plans on getting arrested.
- **Jail Support:** Only required when members have been arrested. The person who fills this role has all the arrestees' contact information and will go to the jail, talk to and work with lawyers, keep track of who got arrested, etc.
- **General Support:** Support roles (people not involved in civil disobedience) are critical to any mass action. Support members provide physical and moral support; know the people in the group by name and description (including special medical information); arrange care of arrestees' cars, personal belongings, etc.; provide transportation to the action; and supply food and water. Support people have additional responsibilities during and after an arrest, as well.

▲

Upper: Camilla Feibelman
— Sierra Student Coalition
Lower: Latosha Moss

*Upper: Tashka Yawanawa
— Indigenous and
Non Indigenous Youth
Lower (left to right):
Dakari Shabazz,
Antar Breaux,
Hakim Sabir*

Support Clusters

A cluster is made up of affinity groups that come together to work on a certain task or part of a larger action. Thus, a cluster might be responsible for blockading an area, locking down together, organizing one day of a multi-day action, or putting together and performing a mass street theater performance. Clusters can be organized around a geographical area, an issue or identity (student cluster or anti-sweatshop cluster, for example) or an action interest (street theater or lockdown, for example).

Spokescouncil

A spokescouncil is the larger organizing structure used in the affinity group model to coordinate a mass action. Each affinity group (or cluster) empowers a 'spoke' (representative) to go to a spokescouncil meeting to decide on important issues for the action. For instance, affinity groups need to decide on a legal/jail strategy, possible tactical issues, meeting places, and many other logistics.

A spokescouncil does not take away an individual affinity group's autonomy; affinity groups make their own decisions about what they want to do on the streets (as long as it fits in with any action guidelines). All decisions in spokescouncils are made by consensus, so all affinity groups have agreed to and are committed to the mass direct action.

CONSENSUS DECISION MAKING

Consensus is a process for group decision making. The input and ideas of all participants are gathered and synthesized to arrive at a final decision that is acceptable to all. Through consensus, people not only work to achieve better solutions, they also work to promote trust and the growth of community.

With consensus, people can and should work through differences to reach a mutually satisfactory position. It is possible for one person's insights or strongly held beliefs to sway the whole group. No ideas are lost; each member's input is valued as part of the solution.

A group committed to consensus may utilize other forms of decision-making (individual, compromise, and majority rules) when appropriate. However, a group that has adopted a consensus model will use that process for any item that brings up a lot of emotions and that concerns people's ethics, politics, and morals.

Consensus does not mean that everyone thinks the decision made is necessarily the best one possible, or even that they are sure it will work. What it does mean is that in coming to that decision, no one felt that her/his position on the matter was misunderstood or not given a proper hearing. Optimally, everyone will think it is the best decision. (This often happens because, when it works, collective intelligence does come up with better solutions than individuals).

For consensus to be a positive experience, it is best if the group has common values, some skill in group process and conflict resolution, commitment and responsibility to the group by its members, and sufficient time for everyone to participate in the process.

In a consensus process, a proposal for resolution is put forward. It is amended and modified through discussion or withdrawn if it seems to be a dead end. During the discussion period, it is important to articulate differences clearly. It is the responsibility of those who are having trouble with a proposal to put forth alternative suggestions. The fundamental right

ANOTHER VOICE

Organizing mass actions goes well beyond what we are doing in the streets. We create a community where people are valued for their ideas, creativity, and their different skills — not as commodities — but as members of a community.

— Jonah Zern

of consensus is that all people are able to express themselves in their own words and of their own will. The fundamental responsibility of consensus is to assure others of their right to speak and be heard. Thus, coercion and trade-offs are replaced with creative alternatives, and compromise is replaced with synthesis.

When a proposal seems to be well understood by everyone and no new changes are asked for, the facilitator(s) will ask if there are any objections or reservations to it. If there are no objections, there can be a call for consensus. If there are still no objections, then after a moment of silence you have your decision. Once consensus appears to have been reached, it really helps to have someone repeat the decision to the group, so that everyone is clear on what has been decided.

If you cannot support a decision that has been reached or is on the verge of being reached, there are several ways for you to express your objections.

- **Non-Support:** "I don't see the need for this, but I'll go along."
- **Reservations:** "I think this may be a mistake but I can live with it."
- **Standing Aside:** "I personally can't do this, but I won't stop others from doing it."
- **Blocking:** "I cannot support this or allow the group to support this. It is immoral." If a final decision violates someone's fundamental moral values, they are obligated to block consensus.

If you Give Me a fish
you have fed me for a day.
If you Teach me to fish
Then you have fed me until
the River is contaminated or
the shoreline seized
for development.
But if you Teach me
to Organize
then whatever the challenge
I can join together
with my peers
And we will fashion
Our own solution.

RICARDO LEVINS MORALES, NORTHLAND POSTER COLLECTIVE

- **Withdrawing from the Group:** If many people express non-support or reservations, or if they stand aside or leave the group, it may not be a viable decision even if no one directly blocks it. This is what is known as a 'lukewarm consensus,' and it is just as desirable as a lukewarm beer or a lukewarm bath.

If consensus is blocked and no new consensus can be reached, then the group stays with whatever the previous decision was on the subject or does nothing, if that is applicable.

There are several roles that, if filled, can help consensus decision making run smoothly.

✓ **Facilitator(s):** Facilitators aid the group in defining decisions that need to be made, help them through the stages of reaching an agreement, keep the meeting moving, focus discussion to the point at hand; make sure everyone has the opportunity to participate, and formulate and test to see if consensus has been reached. Facilitators help to direct the process of the meeting, not its content. They never make decisions for the group. If a facilitator feels too emotionally involved in an issue or discussion and cannot remain neutral in behavior (if not in attitude), then s/he should ask someone to take over the task of facilitation for that agenda item.

✓ **Vibes-Watcher:** Someone besides the facilitator, a vibes-watcher watches and comments on individual and group feelings and patterns of participation. Vibes-watchers need to be especially attuned to the sexism in group dynamics.

NEVA WELTON

✓ **Recorder and Timekeeper:** Recorders take notes on the meeting, especially of decisions made and their means of implementation. Timekeepers keep things on schedule, so that each agenda item can be covered in the time allotted for it. (If discussion runs overtime, the group may or may not decide to contract for more time to finish up.)

Even though individuals take on these roles, all participants in a meeting should be aware of and involved in the issues, process, and feelings of the group, and should share their individual expertise in helping the group to run smoothly and reach a decision. This is especially true when it comes to finding compromise agreements to seemingly contradictory positions.

LINKS

www.directdemocracynow.org
www.actupny.org

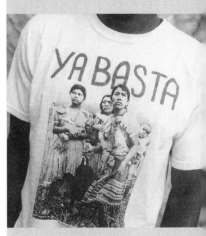
▶ 11.

Yabasta

Mobilizing Global Citizenship Through Mass Direct Action

| YURI THE YABA |

O riginating in 1996, Yabasta is an organization that allows room for new ideas and openness. In Europe in the 1990s, cuts to the welfare state, privatization, and growing immigration amplified the issues of 'disappearing' (marginalization), making Yabasta more relevant to a generation of workers who did not have the same social rights as the previous generation. For Yabasta, the main issues are unemployment and the right to an income, housing, and freedom of movement.

Yabasta's origins are diverse. It is related to the Italian movement of the late '80s and early '90s known as 'squats.' Squats are autonomous occupied social spaces that create opportunities for involvement in radical politics without the institutional mechanisms that tend to privilege old activism in practice and in discourse. Yabasta also has close ties with the Zapatista movement in Mexico. In Spanish 'Yabasta' means 'Enough already!' — an expression taken from the Mexican Zapatista army. Yabasta developed with the intent of translating and applying some of the ideas developed by the Zapatistas in their struggles for the rights of indigenous people in Chiapas to the situation in Europe. Its solidarity with the indigenous

population of Mexico allows Yabasta to materially help their project and to bring ideas and practices back to Western contexts.

Today, Yabasta is a network that unites both the original Yabasta (mostly based in Milan and in the Veneto region in Italy) and the parallel, slightly more recent 1998 movement of 'Tute Bianche' or 'White Overalls.' Since 1999, Yabasta and Tute Bianche have grown through the organizing of major European events, and many countries, such as Spain, Finland, England, Greece, and the United States now have Yabasta and White Overalls nodes.

TIM RUSSO

Anonymous, completely non-hierarchical and non-institutional, the White Overalls movement is based on local structures (squats/occupied social centers). Members wear white chemical suits to emphasize the invisibility of many people whose rights to homes, jobs, and freedom of movement are increasingly threatened.

The basic anonymity of overalls presents a clear message of our leaderless, inclusive solidarity with all marginalized people. The assumption is that an anonymous mass can make themselves visible through mass direct actions, especially if done while wearing white overalls or bright yellow and orange suits. Yellow and orange are reminiscent of prisoners, workfare, and workers in dangerous jobs (often immigrants).

Yabasta is also concerned with freedom of movement. Globalization should not be about the movement of capital and commodities, but rather about promoting the free circulation of humans, regardless of national borders. That is the basic idea behind global citizenship. We don't want division between clandestines and citizens to be added to gender, race, and class divisions in the struggle for people's dignity and against neoliberalism. Everybody should be granted dignity in life — in their housing, healthcare, culture, freedom of movement, and joy. Yabasta believes that our society has the technology and the productive capability to assure dignity and sustain all the world's population.

Yabasta learned from the Zapatistas to play with the media, emphasizing visibility and irony in the actions. Communication is fundamental in today's political scenario; therefore, Yabasta pays particular attention to how direct actions can be communicated and made into a media event.

The forms of civil disobedience we choose reflect the attempt of an involvement from the bottom up, as well as a rethinking of legality. They have to include and attract larger social networks that support, sustain, and defend the actions and at the same time create strong, long-lasting strategies. Our aim is to push the limits of legality as we demonstrate against the presence of the 'globocops' that defend the economic and political leaders who decide our future. Through small actions that include property damage, we seek to enlarge people's knowledge of anti-globalization issues and persuade them to agree on the necessity of such actions. All actions are planned knowing the importance of defending both participants and observers and of making everybody aware of the

risks of committing a crime of property damage. We wear protection against the unnecessary police brutality we have witnessed in all the anti-globalization demonstrations. Inflatable tubes, helmets, and shields made with recycled materials are all limited tools, but they correspond to the kind of political action we practice.

Yabasta is post-ideological, and that's its innovative potential: it privileges strategies and specific actions, rather than affiliating with a historically burdened tradition. Yabasta practices direct action without sectarian ideological divisions and does not try to decide what kind of change each community may want — they can organize and decide for themselves. It has no formal structure; we dress up to protect and support each other to become a critical mass. Our bodies become the only autonomous ground we act with so that we can be heard and given some freedom.

Yuri the Yaba is the collective voice of New York City Yabasta. She is currently living in New York, and interested in connecting and sharing ideas from different traditions of activism in the US, Europe, and Latin America.

▶ 12.

The Total Thrust Is Global Justice

| DREW DELLINGER |

The motivation for everything I do, including activism, is love. We wouldn't be out in the streets protesting if we didn't love the people who are hurting. It's all love: It's love for human beings. It's love for people who are suffering. It's love for the planet and all creation and all creatures.

~

The total thrust is global justice
so we gotta fix the politics
and put a check upon its economics
or before you know it a warrior-poet
may try to upend the
corporate agenda that's
got 'em blind to the real bottom line
It's intense when you sense the only interests
on the docket
are fat cats with Republi-Crats
in their pocket
It's crooked now
just look at how

Drew Dellinger

the pundits are funded
They're devious at CBS and, yes,
they'll choose the news that fits the script unless
I play tricks on the Matrix
(In case you can't guess shit, I'm not to be messed with)
The folks know my art form
comes straight from the heart for 'em
A lyrical storm that departs from the norm
and transforms as I'm givin'
rhymes for the minds in the times that we live in
I can't hang with the anguish
and I don't want my language to languish
'cause there ain't nothing like Drew's hip hop haikus
I got a mandate to disturb the urban landscape
We got tyrannies right here in these States
And you never know when they'll go
Right back to some tactics like COINTELPRO
If we could see through the lies
to see how they brutalize and get cops
to beat speech in the streets and guard sweatshops
I'm endin' these industries
Please can we factor the
effect of the trajectory
This whole place is racist
and sexist from North Dakota down to Texas
with the twenty-first century's
youth in penitentiaries
and the night never seemed this dark
but now half of the stars are behind prison bars

Oh say can you see?
But if we can dream a new day it may be
You had to know the baddest bro
with the phattest flow would shake up the status quo
with my adjectives and my adverbs and my ad libs
— and like Gandhi
protest is my modus operandi
It's like Malcolm and Martin's evolution
with art and revolution
'Cause the total thrust is global justice.

~

*Drew Dellinger lives in
Oakland, where he is founder
and director of Poets for
Global Justice, an
organization promoting
ecology, justice, activism and
cosmology through poetry
and the arts. He is a speaker,
writer, teacher, activist, rap
artist and cofounder of the
band Sweet Acidophilus.*

LINKS

www.soulforce.com

▶ 13.

My Family Wears Black
A Manifesto on Militancy and Anarchism
in the Anti-Globalization Movement

| WARCRY |

DAVID BUTOW

▲

Warcry

This essay represents my perspective only; I do not speak on the behalf of the 'Black Bloc,' or anarchists, or any other segment of the anti-globalization protest movement.

'Black Bloc' is not an organization but a tactic that is historically rooted in the militant anti-fascist movements of Europe. It emerged from the squatting culture in Europe's urban centers and is now widely used in Western European antinuclear and environmental defense movements. Although used in the US for many years, the Black Bloc tactic came to national attention during the anti-WTO protests in Seattle, capturing the imagination of jaded youth everywhere and fueling similar activity in subsequent mass demonstrations. Some who participate consider themselves to be anarchists, but not all.

The wearing of black clothes and facemasks is a major strategy in Black Bloc tactics. The aesthetic is a rejection of materialism and the lure of consumer glorification. In tactical terms, wearing black as a group or a block means that we all look the same, making it harder for police to target individuals. It also provides us some personal safety in the face of potentially violent police troops.

History tells us that we are wise to cover our faces and work in small groups, to guard against infiltrators. The facemasks provide anonymity and protection against police and intelligence cameras in the streets. Those who accuse us of hiding behind masks fail to understand the reality of a high-tech surveillance state and the government's capacity for disruption and activist harassment, a la COINTELPRO (the FBI Counter Intelligence Programs of the 1960s that basically tore those movements apart).

Occasionally, someone will take it upon herself or himself to try and tear off our masks. I would encourage such hostility to be redirected to tearing off the mask that the government wears when it claims to uphold our rights at protests, even as it conducts mass preemptive arrests, declares 'no-protest zones,' and generally makes a mockery of our rights. Tear off the masks of those who claim to serve the public interest, while hiding behind massive public relations machines and corporate sponsors. Or better yet, undo the myth of fairness and objectivity and tear off the mask that the media wears while cheerleading murderous government policies and destructive corporate practices. I would encourage people to tear off the mask that they themselves wear when they fail to acknowledge the level of damage corporate greed has inflicted on the natural treasures of this continent and the institutionalized brutality it visits daily on the human spirit. These are the masks worth permanently stripping away.

PROPERTY DESTRUCTION AND MOVEMENT POLITICS

People who criticize politically motivated property destruction as violent must think broken windows can feel pain and scream like people do when they are shot by rubber bullets. During the WTO

protests in Seattle, police opened fire with very little warning on a peaceful crowd — before anything got smashed in downtown Seattle. A 6-year-old was shot in the face; a 50-year-old woman still can't see out of her left eye. Violence is when someone gets hurt, and the only people perpetrating violence during the WTO protests were the police.

Some insist that the message must be delivered in a way that doesn't jeopardize the message itself. They choose to lock arms, block roads, etc., and they deserve respect and support for putting themselves in vulnerable positions and accepting the consequences of their civil disobedience. But no matter how the message is delivered, accepting diversity in the movement is the most critical aspect to consider. No one group should set the guidelines for the protests or claim ownership of the movement. As anarchists, we do not advocate mindless destruction, and we simply ask that the movement be open to a diversity of tactics.

It seems incredibly easy to find conflict within the movement — even among friends and within oneself. What hopes keep you from flying apart? What common threats are we collectively facing? What human rights are we all asserting together? It is easy to find obstacles, and it is important to find solutions and assert our common ground — because that is where we take our stand.

Third World peasants, vulnerable in their poverty, generally cannot challenge the ultra-powerful multinationals. Neither can the ecology and wildlife, which remain completely mute and defenseless. We are the voices of the voiceless, and we must be loud, because the men in suits high up in their office towers don't hear the screams of misery below or see the wasted ruins of the Earth. So, we attack their symbols. It's the least we can do.

INTERNATIONAL SOLIDARITY AND POLITICAL VIOLENCE

In Europe, activists successfully addressed the problem of violent and nonviolent forms of protest by designating a separate color-coded march for each group, thereby accommodating the diversity in tactics. The blue group, for example, was the militant segment and had their own route; the pink group, who was not militant, had a different route. One group threw Molotov cocktails; the other played Samba music. The different groups ended up complementing each other. There was still conflict, of course, but it was comparatively minimal since everyone's tactics were — if not sanctioned — at least not impeded or condemned from the outset.

Rock throwing is a tradition unique to European protests. All it takes is a pickaxe to loosen up the cobblestone streets, which then become an element of battle in confronting police barricades, tanks, and riot cops. Some do not categorize corporate property destruction as violent, but would throwing rocks at cops be considered violent? Some would unequivocally answer: Yes! Some would say: No! Some say cops are instruments of the very forces of destruction we are fighting desperately to change. Some would argue that we can't fight evil structures by replicating their values. Others would argue that cops never hesitate to use violence on civilians and do not deserve to be respected like other human beings. Some would argue that the police are working-class humans stuck in a dehumanizing system, while others would argue that police are the prison guards of society and need to be overcome.

Is it more important to change ideas than throw rocks? Is it important to do both? For some, an attack on police is an attack on the police state. For others, it is less useful to fight the cops than to directly confront the lawmakers and the corporate puppet masters.

DAVID BUTOW

Was the Vietnamese teenager who picked up anti-aircraft artillery and blew up an incoming US bomber plane being violent? Or was it self-defense? Were the Zapatistas being violent in their armed uprising against lifetimes of exploitation and enforced misery? Or was it an expression of human dignity to forcefully reject the conditions of poverty that globalization and neo-imperialism perpetuate? There are no easy answers — only personal choices. And the arguments will rage on.

MEDIA

Why does the media focus on anarchists trashing but doesn't find newsworthy the fact that the WTO and its ilk are trashing the planet daily on a massive scale? Why is it that they blubber over Niketown's broken windows but don't find newsworthy the fact that 14-year-old Vietnamese girls work 12-hour days for subsistence wages, inhaling toxic dust in Nike-contracted factories?

Windows can be replaced, but old-growth forests cannot. Neither can the lungs of a 14-year-old Vietnamese girl nor the lives of those who toil and labor mutely, as vampire capitalists suck the lifeblood out of them and fatten themselves with immense windfall profits. Millions make do without adequate healthcare and have only insecure, fearful futures for themselves and their children.

The media rarely gives in-depth coverage to these real issues, regardless of whether anything gets smashed or not. Most often, protests are ignored unless there is something sensational about them — like black-clad youth smashing corporate property. After the WTO protests, one newsman said in reference to the window-smashing, "We decided to give coverage to the legitimate protests." In other words, anyone who was protesting in a fashion that he considered illegitimate would be denied coverage. The media deliberately decides what to legitimize and what to ignore. Apparently, our crisis of our democracy is not a legitimate enough issue to cover. The lack of a democratic media hinders democracy, so when I see a major newspaper stand toppled in the street during a protest, I have trouble mustering sympathy.

ANARCHISTS

We are your problem children. That's because your institutionalized injustice *is* the problem. Centuries of abuse by so-called legitimate authorities have left a bad taste on the anarchist palate. Maybe it was the mass witch burning that killed women by the thousands in Europe and pre-Colonial America. That was rationalized by the authority figures of the day, was it not? The number of Native Americans killed on this blood-soaked continent outnumbers the holocaust victims of Germany. This is history not taught in our schools. Slavery was an economic cornerstone in this country, not unlike the corporate feudalism of today. For decades blacks were not recognized as human beings. This government, the most technologically advanced superpower in the world, rained near nuclear-strength bombs on a peasant population in the Third World for over a decade, killing three million people. Authority has a history of coercive abuse, and that doesn't appear to be changing. And this is the law that expects our respect? We say: No. We say: FUCK YOU.

Call no man master. Let each man remain his own master.
Do not go to the offices of bureaucrats or the noisy
chambers of parliaments in the vain hope for the words of
freedom. Listen rather to the voices which come from
below, even if they come through the bars of the prison cell.
— Eisee Reclus, Russian revolutionary (1885)

Anarchism is freedom from tyranny of thought and habit. It is the rejection of the legitimacy of a coercive social order based on violence. Anarchism conceives of a society that allows for the conditions where humankind's potential has the chance to realize itself and not be enslaved in thought and deed. Humans have always longed for this freedom, even if some of us have never known it. The seriousness of revolution is alive in these nameless faces behind masks — bright eyes, full of daring and resolve, anonymous figures in tighter solidarity than some of us will ever express with our real families.

CONCLUSION

Revolution transforms the individual as well as the world. Self-liberation occurs as we reclaim and realize our power by expressing it. We have nowhere to put our faith but in the courage of each other. This global resistance is really a global hunger for democracy and an assertion of human dignity and self-determination. It seeks liberation within militarized zones, within industrial nations, and within imposing hierarchies that have robbed people across the world of their power to shape and direct their own lives. This global resistance is demanding effective change and effective democracy in the face of overwhelming state and corporate control and tyranny.

▼

Warcry's home base is New York City. She is a poet, anarchist, and an environ-mental activist who has participated in tree-sits in the redwood forest. For the past two years, Warcry has participated in nearly all of the anti-globalization actions around the world.

▶ 14.

COINTELPRO

Infiltrating the Anti-Corporate Globalization Movement

| JIM REDDEN |

They're at it again. Twenty-five years after government officials promised to stop spying on peaceful political protesters, law enforcement officials are openly bragging about infiltrating the emerging anti-corporate globalization movement. This domestic spying violates federal, state, and local prohibitions passed in the wake of public outrage over the FBI's Counter-Intelligence Programs, commonly called COINTELPRO.

Operating from August 1956 to April 1971, COINTELPRO monitored and harassed a broad range of political activists, including communists, pacifists, and civil rights protesters. The FBI authorized over 2,300 actions as part of these operations, including 715 that were specifically designed to disrupt organizations. Although created by FBI Director J. Edgar Hoover, presidents from both political parties authorized them — just as the current operations, which began under Democrat Bill Clinton and are continuing under Republican George W. Bush.

Here are the major COINTELPRO operations:

- COINTELPRO-CPUSA was launched in August 1956 against the Communist Party USA and 'Communist-influenced people,' including numerous civil rights leaders. Tactics ranged from identifying party members and disrupting meetings with calls for violence to instigating police raids on party offices around the country.

- The SWP Disruption Program began in October 1961, targeting the Socialist Workers Party. It also gathered information on organizations that cosponsored events with the Marxist splinter group.

- The Klan/White Hate Groups operation authorized in September 1964 was directed at 17 Klan organizations and 9 other hate groups. Informants were elected to top leadership positions in over half the Klan units under investigation.

- The Black Nationalist Hate Groups operation, started in August 1967, targeted groups ranging from the Black Panther Party to the Southern Christian Leadership Conference and included most African-American student organizations on college campuses.

- The New Left program, approved in May 1968, collected information on youth and antiwar groups, ranging from Students for a Democratic Society to the Women's International League for Peace and Freedom and all employees and students at Antioch University.

Other intelligence agencies spied on political dissidents, too. Major operations included:

- The Watch List Program, started in 1967 by the National Security Agency, collected "any information on a continuing basis" concerning foreigners attempting to influence US peace and Black Power groups.

- Operation CHAOS, created by the Central Intelligence Agency in 1967, monitored all "radical students, antiwar activists, draft resisters and deserters, black nationalists, anarchists, and assorted New Leftists traveling abroad."

- Project MERRIMACK, also created in 1967, used CIA agents to infiltrate antiwar and civil rights groups based in Washington, DC and gathered information about the leadership, funding, activities, and policies of the targeted groups.

- Project RESISTANCE, also created in 1967, was a broad CIA effort to obtain general background information on radical groups across the country, particularly on college and university campuses.

- The Pentagon also operated continuous counterintelligence investigations to obtain information on "subversive personalities, groups, or organizations" and their "influence on urban populations" throughout the 1960s. Targets included dissident elements, the civil rights movement, the anti-Vietnam/anti-draft movements, and prominent persons who were friendly with the leaders or "sympathetic with their plans."

- The most out-of-control COINTELPRO operation targeted such African-American political organizations as the Black Panther Party. Agent provocateurs helped federal, state, and local law enforcement officials set up black activists on bogus charges, occasionally prompting violent confrontations with the police. Twenty-eight leaders and members were killed over an 18-month period, incapacitating the party.
- Stewart Albert, a longtime peace activist, says the government infiltrators undercut the unified antiwar/civil rights movement. "The informants changed the entire culture of the movement," Albert says. "It started out very open and trusting, but after we realized we had been infiltrated, people became paranoid, fearful, and distrustful. Before too long, the movement became just like the society it was protesting."

A US Senate subcommittee, chaired by Frank Church, exposed this operation in 1976, prompting government leaders to promise they would stop spying on political dissidents. But the following recent events show these promises are being broken:

- Delta Force commandos dressed up like protesters and videotaped anti-WTO demonstrators in Seattle in November 1999.
- Federal, state, and local police agencies infiltrated groups planning protests at the April 2000 World Bank/IMF meeting in Washington, DC.

- Using information provided by US agencies, Canadian authorities prevented 600 suspected activists from crossing into Ontario to protest the Organization of American States meeting in June 2000.
- Minneapolis police had local activists under surveillance before the July 2000 meeting of the International Society of Animal Genetics.
- Federal, state, and local police spied on protesters at both the Republican National Convention and the Democratic National Convention, targeting leaders such as John Sellers of the Ruckus Society for prosecution on inflated charges.
- High-tech surveillance systems, including airborne cameras operated by the National Imagery and Mapping Agency, tracked protesters during the January 2001 inauguration of President George W. Bush.

These events make the Church Committee's conclusions relevant today:

> *Too many people have been spied upon by too many Government agencies and too much information has been collected. The Government has often undertaken the secret surveillance of citizens on the basis of their political beliefs, even when those beliefs posed no threat of violence or illegal acts on behalf of a hostile foreign power. The Government, operating primarily through secret informants, but also using other intrusive techniques such as wiretaps, microphone 'bugs,' surreptitious mail*

Jim Redden began writing for Oregon's underground press during in the 1960s and is senior staff writer for the Portland Tribune. He is the author of Snitch Culture: How Citizens Are Turned into the Eyes and Ears of the State.

opening, and break-ins, has swept in vast amounts of information about the personal lives, views, and associations of American citizens. Investigations of groups deemed potentially dangerous — and even of groups suspected of associating with potentially dangerous organizations — have continued for decades, despite the fact that those groups did not engage in unlawful activity. Groups and individuals have been harassed and disrupted because of their political views and their lifestyles. Investigations have been based upon vague standards whose breadth made excessive collection inevitable.

And if history is any guide, we do not yet know how much government surveillance is currently underway. Remember that the Church Committee report was issued 20 years after the first COINTELPRO operation was launched.

▶ 15.

Co-opting the Radical Instinct

A Warning

| TOM HAYDEN |

▲

Tom Hayden

Ruckus Society Action Camp, Malibu (Summer 2000)

I think that you all might want to know something about how the other side sees you. There's a study done by the Cattlemen's Society. Now, you may think they're an irrelevant, marginal group, but they're quite crucial to the frontier mentality that built this great country on the backs of the native people. They are a big special interest group, and they pay good money to find out who these activists are. A few years ago they did a study. The question was: How do we contain and stop this direct action movement? It wasn't called the direct action movement then; it was the civil disobedience movement, the protesters, the environmentalists, all the rabble that they were concerned about at the time.

They created a chart. At one end were the radicals, defined as people who believe that the system itself has to be changed. A radical would be anybody who understands that globalization is a system with many fronts and many issues. Their prescription for the radicals was to isolate and discredit them, not because there was something inherently radical in their behavior, but because they were pointing out that it was a system. So, the first goal, they said, was to discredit the radical analysis.

| 73 |

The second group on the spectrum were the idealists. These are people who want to give the system a chance. They believe in the same social justice values that the radicals do, but they're idealistic; they don't have a cold, cynical view that nothing is possible under the system. So, it's extremely important, the study said, that the idealists don't become radicals. In order to keep this from happening, you raise the stakes of radicalism so that people are afraid to become radical, because they then get smeared, discredited, and worse. You have to give the idealists occasional victories in order to keep their hope in the system alive.

Third on this continuum came the pragmatists. The pragmatists are former idealists who've won some victories, who start to believe that the system works. So, they said, it's extremely important for the idealists to have victories — not because of justice, but because that way they become pragmatists. And you want the pragmatists to be able to say: See? The system works. Be pragmatic.

And the final part of the spectrum — the culmination of your future, if you follow this plan — is that you can become an opportunist. An opportunist is a former pragmatist. An opportunist, they said, is a pragmatist who gets attracted to the money, the glamour, the status, and the power. And then they had a whole workshop on how this could be done. How to discredit the radicals, cultivate the idealists, make them pragmatists, and then find the opportunists among the pragmatists. And there — you have the story of my generation, the 60s generation.

You have millions of people who have radical instincts but little expectation, who have lowered their expectation. You have millions of people who are former idealists, who have become pragmatists. And you have plenty of people who are opportunists.

My question is: How can you break this cycle? It's the most important cycle to break. You can't break the cycle of poverty; you can't break the cycle of violence; you can't break the cycle of corporate expansion; you can't break the cycle of the arms race; you can't break the cycle of imprisonment, if you don't break the cycle by which radicals are isolated, idealists are turned into pragmatists, and pragmatists into opportunists. I have not found an answer to this problem, but I'm here to tell you it is *the* problem. And you are its answer.

▼

Tom Hayden cofounded Students for a Democratic Society (SDS) in 1959. After the 1968 Democratic National Convention in Chicago, he was indicted with the Chicago Seven and later acquitted. Tom Hayden is currently a state senator from Los Angeles and has authored over 175 measures, including animal welfare, campaign finance, education, environmental, prison reform, and worker safety initiatives.

Amy Goodman

▶ 16.

Democracy Now!
Challenging Power on the Air

| AMY GOODMAN |

Today, the most powerful global corporations in the world are the corporate media — those in telecommunications. They are powerful in two ways: they are very wealthy, and they are shaping and determining how we view the world. Even though it seems that we have more channels and more ways to get information than ever before, just a few corporations own most media outlets.

My goal with Democracy Now!, and locally at WBAI in New York, is to open up the airwaves to those people who are generally locked out of the mainstream discourse but who represent the majority point of view in the world. The corporate view, which is a tiny minority of the viewpoints of the world, is the one that we continually hear as a kind of drumbeat. According to Noam Chomsky, hearing corporate, mainstream information over and over inevitably leads one to believe that their view represents the way things are and should be. Democracy Now!'s motto is: "The exception to the rulers."

I've always felt that as journalists we're not here to cozy up to power, but to challenge it. For example, on Election Day 2000, President Clinton called the radio station to put out a message to the people to get out and vote for Hillary Rodham Clinton and for Al

Gore. Since we had him on the line, we decided to ask him a series of questions. We grilled him for 30 minutes. The next day the White House called and said I would be banned from the White House, that they would not cooperate with us. They really were angry, because they said I had broken the ground rules. Which were what? We had made no deal. But in reality, most journalists have an unspoken rule with those in power not to challenge them — a self-censorship that is commonplace and destructive.

The idea was that Clinton could call lots of radio stations — around 40 — and automatically have a platform that he could speak from. Well, we don't provide that platform. We are not here to applaud politicians but to challenge them. And that's what we did, naturally. A journalist ordinarily prepares for a year to have a 30-minute interview with the president of the United States. They didn't give us any notice. And it's deliberate — they don't want you to prepare; they just want to get their message out.

Well, we cover many movements and talk to people every day about the issues they care deeply about, so it wasn't too hard to come up with questions. At the time they were: Will you grant executive clemency to Leonard Peltier? What about the sanctions against Iraq that have killed 5,000 people a month? What about racial profiling? What about a moratorium on the death penalty? What about the bombing of Viequez? The majority of people on Viequez are fiercely opposed to it, and yet the US navy is not only bombing but renting Viequez out so that allies can bomb them, too. Clinton wasn't pleased. He said I was combative, hostile, and at times disrespectful. Well, I wasn't. I was courteous. But I also did ask him a series of questions that any journalist should ask.

independent
media center

We don't go on bended knee to power. We don't treat these people as royalty. It's our responsibility to challenge them, to go to where the silence is and say something. I would go to White House press briefings and ask why the US government was pushing another weapons sale to Indonesia. The other journalists would just roll their eyes, as if to say: Oh, please. The one who asks the questions about Timor. Well, Indonesia was occupying Timor and had killed a third of its population using US weapons. I would continually ask these questions, certainly objectively. Very appropriate. After all, it is one of the worst genocides of the 20th century.

The word "media" comes from "medium," meaning "something through which information passes unmediated." So our responsibility is to get the information out — to report on the experiences people are having so that the listener, the viewer, the reader, can decide for themselves. The question is: Which way is the video camera pointed? Which way is the microphone pointed? Is it pointed inside at the World Trade Organization, or outside at the people who are protesting? That's where we want it: outside, where the majority voices are.

I encourage people to take microphones and video cameras with them when they go to protests, to demonstrations, and when they're out on the streets. First of all, we have to document — it's our safety. Second, when we document what's happening, it puts people on notice that they're not alone. We must also document to show how people are building a better world and chronicle each step of the way. We're the new watchdogs. Video cameras and microphones can be a powerful tool of social change.

ANOTHER VOICE

Bobby Seal of the Black Panthers once said that if the Panthers were organizing now, they wouldn't be toting guns, they would be using digital cameras and laptops. That's because whoever controls access to information influences people's minds, and that's the next battleground.

— Samuel Delgado

I see things as pretty straightforward. Do we want to represent the sword or the shield? That should be the guide for people when they make their decisions. In the case of US foreign policy, we provide weapons to countries like Indonesia that oppress their own people — that's the sword. A tape recorder, a video camera, a microphone — that's the shield. To reflect what is happening is a revolutionary act.

It's not always easy to be the shield. But all I have to do is imagine myself sitting with people in power and then imagine myself sitting in Timor in 1991, when I witnessed the Indonesian military kill more than 250 Timorese. Again and again, I've learned that if you can be grounded in what you believe is right and not doubt your experiences, that will be your greatest guide and keep you on the right path. It will keep your shield strong.

▼

Amy Goodman hosts "Democracy Now!" produced by Pacifica Radio. It is considered one of the few effective sources of honest analysis and reporting in the United States. Her work embodies outrageous courage, tireless audacity, and a mighty passion for community radio.

LINKS

www.pacifica.org

▶ 17.

Force Real Change

Strategies for Broadening the Movement

| JUAN GONZALEZ |

▲

Juan Gonzalez

JERRY BAUER

I t is very important for young activists to study the history of popular movements in order to avoid repeating the same mistakes. But at the same time, they shouldn't be constrained by the advice of elders. Very often the elders who interpret that history are a little bit ossified in their views of what are the best tactics and strategies to use at any given time. What is important is to learn the lessons of how other movements rose, what caused them to decline, the internal problems that they could or could not overcome, as well as the external repression and conditions of the society that led to their decline. For instance, most activists today don't know that it was the Students for a Democratic Society (SDS) who coined the term 'participatory democracy.' It was one of their most important principles and played a big role in how SDS grew. It meant everyone had to be involved in the meetings and decisions and was an attempt to get away from a hierarchical type of leadership that had become so prevalent in American society. Eventually it became unwieldy, because there are limitations in every form of political organization. Knowing what happened with SDS, Student Nonviolent Coordinating Committee (SNCC), the Wobblies, and the Populist movement provides enormous lessons for the new social movements of this decade.

Sometimes, in movements, there's a tendency to fall prey to what I call 'sugar-coated bullets:' thinking that doing the same thing over and over again is going to be successful in the same way. That didn't happen in Seattle, but it could happen in the future. The most important thing about Seattle was that it caught the power structures by surprise. They had no idea that this movement had been gathering and was at such a high level of development. They were totally unprepared to deal with the militancy of the young people, the mass numbers that the labor movement brought out, the rebelliousness of the Third World delegates within the assembly, and the non-governmental organizations (NGOs) that bridged the ties between those countries and provided information and analysis. All this is very important, because many Third World governments were opposed to globalization but had been convinced that there was no way to fight it. For them to suddenly find out that there were all of these Americans who were upset about it gave them strength. At a certain point, they realized that there was a movement of resistance here that would aid them in their struggle.

Now the forces of repression are fully awake, and they know exactly the danger posed if this anti-globalization movement grows. Ever since Seattle, they have worked overtime to offer as many carrots as they can to the NGOs, and to make some sort of peace with the labor movement — basically to divide up the opposition. They've also sought to repress much more strongly, with much more sophistication, those who continue to mount demonstrations in the streets. They're following all the leaders and what demonstrations they're going to next — preparing for them, because they are determined to prevent another Seattle.

The fact is, we don't really need another Seattle; we don't need to go around the world and replicate it over and over again. You have to be able to change your tactics. The movement is now at the stage where we need to force *real* change. All the things that have been accomplished already as a result of Seattle are amazing. The dominant forces in the advanced countries are far more aware of how important Seattle was than are the corporate media in America, who have no idea of the impact Seattle had on the power structures. In essence, Seattle exposed and delegitimized the neoliberal model of globalization. It was a key moment. But the reality is that the kind of historical moment that happened in Seattle doesn't come around two or three times a year. It comes around sometimes once in a generation. In my opinion, disrupting a city is no longer where the movement is at — it's got to broaden.

The problem in the US now is how to translate the successes into an ongoing movement that reaches wider and wider sectors of American society: the African-American and Latino communities, and the labor movement. That doesn't mean you don't do demonstrations. But any movement for radical social change needs millions of people, not just thousands. Rather than becoming purely a movement of middle class and educated folks, it needs to reach the grassroots.

I think that the issues of ecological devastation and genetic engineering offer the greatest potentials for broadening the movement. Ecological devastation affects everyone, though poor communities often bear the brunt of its effects. And the dangers of genetic engineering, along with a lack of public oversight and

ANOTHER **VOICE**

Understanding the reasons for the low level of color and what can be learned from it is absolutely crucial if we are to make Seattle's promise of a new, international movement against imperialist globalization come true.

— Elizabeth
(Betita) Martinez

scrutiny of its development, are going to have an enormous impact on the rich/poor divide. If the young people who understand all of this, who are knowledgeable and have been struggling with these issues can translate them and get them into working class and poor communities, I think they're going to be able to mobilize huge numbers of people in the future. And that's what's going to empower this movement for real change.

▼

Journalist Juan Gonzalez has covered a wide range of national events as a staff columnist with The New York Daily News *and as co-host of "Democracy Now!," with Amy Goodman. He is known for his hard-hitting reporting on the labor movement, race relations, and problems of the inner city.*

▶ 18.

Weeks of Rage
Taking On Community Justice

| PECOLIA MANIGO |

Pecolia Manigo (far left)

Born from the Aaron Williams case, Third Eye Movement (3EM), currently in the process of reforming and changing its name, is a youth-led community organization opposing police brutality and the criminalization of youth. Aaron Williams was an African-American youth who was brutally beaten, pepper sprayed, and arrested. He needed hospitalization, but instead of providing him with healthcare, Marc Andaya (a police officer with a long record of misconduct) threw Aaron out on the street, where he died. 3EM developed a campaign that brought together youth, community, churches, and grassroots organizations for the single purpose of firing Marc Andaya. Our campaign was a success.

After the Aaron Williams campaign, we started to do "Know Your Rights" trainings, because we saw that a lot youth needed this education. And not just like: 'I have the right to remain silent,' but also on how to assert your rights, how to deal with police, and know what police can and cannot do. We created a "Know Your Rights" pocket card, so that if people had an encounter with the police, they could pull it out and say: Okay... Wait a minute. You're not supposed to do such and such.

Our biggest campaign was against Proposition 21 (Prop 21), a law passed in California in March 2000 that forces youth as young as 14 into the adult criminal justice system. Prop 21 also expands the mandatory 'Three strikes you're out' sentencing rules and drastically reduces what is necessary for police to target somebody as a gang member. It allows police to place these so-called suspects into the California gang database — a database that contains more than half of the African-American males in Los Angeles who are under age 25. (Obviously, half of the under-25, African-American male population is not in gangs!)

COURTESY OF SCHOOLS NOT JAILS

Our angle was to expose who was behind the initiative, who wrote it, and who funded it. We found out it was Pete Wilson (then Mayor of San Francisco), and behind him were a whole lot of corporations, such as Hilton, Pacific Gas and Electric (PG&E), as well as some very rich donors.

We hooked up with a bunch of other organizations for this one: The Data Center for Research, Youth Force, Schools Not Jails Coalition, We Interrupt This Message, Youth Organizing Communities, and others. We did phone jams; we did a sit-in at the Hilton Hotel; and we converged on PG&E's brown-bag luncheon with the CEO and employees. Then, about three weeks before the vote on Prop 21, we planned a statewide demonstration called "Weeks of Rage."

For three weeks, before, during, and after the Prop 21 vote, simultaneous actions took place throughout the state — all the way from Eureka to San Diego. We learned that when you do these actions collaboratively and consecutively, you get a lot more publicity, especially when the actions increase in power. Like, a walkout is really high on the publicity scale, whereas a vigil isn't. Both will get you attention, but a walkout will prove a point and hit your target in its pockets.

We did a very, very big concert in Oakland on President's Day when there was no school. So everybody came out. We rocked it, right there at the city hall in Oakland all day long. That morning all the people you wouldn't necessarily say are youth got arrested to show their solidarity with the youth movement. The rest of that week there were simultaneous walkouts with San Diego and LA County. There were so many different things: vigils, targets on corporations, banner drops, and teach-ins.

We took over one of the worst looking schools in San Francisco — a continuation school for students who are at risk. We had a rally and a freedom school for two days. And everybody was like: Whoa! You guys took over a school. Even though the press thought we were crazy and the police really hated us, the school administrators were down with us. They were down with the youth movement and wanted to see us succeed, because they didn't want to see more money go into building all the juvenile rehabilitation facilities that were going to be needed if Prop 21 won.

Then 1,500 people took over the Hilton Hotel. Basically, we were ready to stay until someone got us Mr. Hilton on the phone or the manager came and talked to us. We were not leaving until we got something. Eventually 200 people got arrested. Twenty-three were youth; one of them was me. Even though we lost the Prop 21 campaign, we learned a lot about standing up for what we believe in.

Our group is new and young and fresh, and we're just learning organizational development. After four years of miraculous success, we are changing our name to reflect the shifts in the organization. Our movement was building internally, and we recognized that we needed to develop ourselves as individuals and to reorganize so that we could be more effective. Now we need to be really deliberate about consciousness and solidarity. We have to be careful or we won't continue to build this movement. We have to define ourselves a little bit more: What are our boundaries? What does it mean to build allies? And how does that work from a state, national, and international level? If we can do that, we will succeed.

▼

Having been evicted from her home at age 12, as gentrification began to take over the Mission District in San Francisco, Pecolia Manigo started organizing on homeless issues. These days, she is the co-trainer of Youth Power, an after-school program that trains middle school students to be community leaders. She is an all around, 24/7 souljah and organizer dedicated to serving her community.

▶ 19.

The Prison Industrial Complex

Exposing the Interlocking Systems of Oppression

| CRITICAL RESISTANCE |

The prison industrial complex (PIC) is a multifaceted system that designates prisons as a solution to social, political, and economic problems. The PIC intersects with and depends upon the oppressive systems of racism, classism, sexism, and homophobia. It encompasses human rights violations, the death penalty, exploitative industry and labor, policing, courts, media, community disenfranchisement, the imprisonment of political prisoners and prisoners of war, and the elimination of dissent.

To fully describe the PIC, we have to look holistically at what makes it function as it does. For example, the boom in prison construction can be attributed to, among other factors: the massive increase in the number of people sentenced to prison terms with the implementation of the war on drugs; the repression of radical movements by people of color for self-determination; and the anti-imperialist struggles of the '60s, '70s, and '80s. The war on drugs and national and local efforts to destroy radical political movements led to an increased police presence in communities of color and poor communities, higher arrest rates, and longer prison sentences. The boom is also fueled by dramatic and racist reporting about crime, delinquency, and rebellion that create a culture of fear. It continues to be acceptable and desirable to many (upper class and white people) to lock people (primarily people of color, youth, and poor people) in cages for longer and longer periods of time, in the interest of 'public safety.' It is precisely the multifaceted nature of the PIC that makes it so powerful and destructive. In order to change the system, we have to see it for all that it is and recognize what drives and shapes it.

Opposing the PIC means we must redefine the dominant culture's notions of public safety. We must challenge the idea that police, prisons, and the court system serve the people who are not in power or making concessions to the power structure. At the same time, we must create an alternate idea of security, based on the safety of the people most affected by the PIC and the values of the system that perpetuate it.

RACISM, GLOBALIZATION, AND THE EXPANSION OF PRISONS

The United States currently imprisons up to two million people. More than five million people are presently under some form of supervision within the criminal justice system. According to US Department of Justice statistics, by 1992 one out of three Black men between the ages of 20 and 29 (and in some cities such as Baltimore and Washington, DC, 50 percent of Black men between the ages of 18 and 35) were under some form of criminal justice supervision. The Department of Justice predicts that at the current rates of incarceration, a Black male born in 1991 has a 29 percent chance of going to prison at least once during his lifetime (Dyer, 2000).

Women represent the fastest-rising prison population. Since 1980, the number of women incarcerated in the US has risen by almost 400 percent. According to the May 1994 issue report of the Women's Economic Agenda Project, 54 percent of women in prison are women of color (prisonactivist.org).

Furthermore, racism continues to be a major determining factor in the United States, manifested by the policies, programs, and doctrines of white supremacy. This institutionalized racism is reinforced by a capitalist, profit-driven economic system. At the dawn of the 21st century, the shift from monopoly capitalism to global capitalism is the defining phenomenon. In this period, nation-states have become less autonomous and have surrendered more of their control to multinational bodies, such as the World Bank and the International Monetary Fund. Deindustrialization, technological breakthroughs, and global job competition have resulted in unemployment, underemployment, and poverty, particularly in people of color communities (Holt, 2000).

As states scramble to stake their claims in the globalizing world, "the rise of prisons in the United States constitutes a principal factor in the future 'globalization circulation models,' because prison-building is state-building at its least contested... Racism, as exercised through criminal laws that target certain kinds of people in centers where people of color are disproportionately crowded, is structural — not individual nor incidental" (Smith 1996; Gilmore 1999). "Through prison export, both US and non-US racist practices can become determining forces in places nominally 'free' of white supremacy. Indeed, as with the twentieth, the problem of the twenty-first century is freedom — the de-coupling of power and difference" (Gilmore 2000).

The implications for organizing resistance against both globalization and the PIC are significant. With burgeoning international movements against globalization — and the potential for inclusion in those movements of a wide array of related arguments against other systems of oppression and domination — it would be ideal to work hard to understand the areas of overlap and interaction. That said, it is also essential that movements against globalization (which in the US are largely white) recognize the need to challenge white supremacy as well as class and gender privilege within themselves. Movements need to develop a political stance that addresses globalization through an understanding of both domestic and international injustices and uses of power. Movements against the PIC can benefit from recognizing the exportability of the US prison model (as Gilmore describes it) and prepare to take on not only a domestic struggle, but also all the international contexts in which work against the PIC (especially the American model) will become necessary and related to work in the US.

LEARNING FROM THE PAST

From the mid-1960s to the mid-1970s, the Black Panther Party, the Young Lords, the American Indian Movement and many other young radicals in the United States called for revolution. They asserted that the US was committed to remaining a racist, capitalist, sexist, homophobic society that exploited people of color and the working class, domestically and internationally. Therefore, they reasoned, it must be completely and systematically changed.

Bolstered by the success of national liberation movements in the Third World, predominantly youth-led organizations fostered a revolutionary movement in the United States (Jones, 1998; Torres and Velazquez, 1998). Grassroots organizing, mass demonstrations, and direct action were frequent tactics. Counter-institutions (such as food cooperatives, bookstores, and liberation schools) and programs providing services to disenfranchised communities were created.

Resistance to the system became the driving force behind a new popular youth culture. Today, the memories of that era continue to give many who lived through that period a sense of hope.

However, we must not romanticize the past. Instead, let us look at what lessons can be learned and applied to contemporary struggles. By the late-1970s the revolution was effectively crushed. Leaders were killed, driven into exile, and incarcerated due to the corrupt actions of local and federal law enforcement agencies (Churchill and Vander Wall, 1988). The idealism and hopes many held for a new society disintegrated into cynicism and disillusion.

We can learn from the mistakes that radical organizations made strategically, structurally, and in organizational and personal relationships. Not to minimize the state's interest and role in defeating a potential US revolution, some of the primary difficulties youth-based revolutionary organizations faced were internal. Strategic inflexibility, authoritarian and cult-of-personality leadership, sexism, homophobia, racism, and elitism plagued youth organizing (as they continue to, though perhaps not as frequently). All of these factors contributed to easier infiltration and disruption by the state.

Now, perhaps more than at any other historical period, youth activists have the added task of creating organizations that will counter the self-hatred, devaluation of life, and consumerist mentality that has befallen poor communities and communities of color. Democratic and accountable organizations are critical to building trust and defeating the political cynicism that is rampant among poor youth and youth of color.

CONCLUSION

Prisons are not an answer to crime. We must learn to critique prisons within the context of power. We must learn to critique power. The nature of the debate about prisons and policing in US society is shifting toward a moral view that although prisons are still necessary for some 'bad' people, laws and policies putting people behind bars are not fair and should be reformed. Some activists and policymakers are using this shift to advocate for changes while the political climate is ripe.

The movement against the PIC runs the risk of being shaped by easy victories or simplified struggles that do not recognize and fight the entirety of the system — a system shaped and defined by racism, classism, sexism, and homophobia. We need to understand that we have no option but to fight and continue to fight, until all of those intersecting systems that jeopardize our survival no longer exist.

One important place to begin is to push the movement to a more sophisticated and holistic analysis of race, class, and gender. We cannot allow ourselves to do short-term work that undermines our long-term vision and goals or to rely on the same systems of oppression and domination that sustain and drive the PIC to influence mainstream voters. In order to do this work, we have to continue to create spaces for people with diverging points of view to have honest, facilitated dialogue and disagreement about directions the movement against the PIC will take.

Since we are so frequently asked what we are 'for' rather than 'against,' the struggle against prisons, police, repression, punishment, and the criminalization of entire communities must demonstrate a clear vision of a viable world without the PIC. This is another immediate and important site of definition and activist work. One way to define and shape what we are for is to create a culture of resistance or a culture and society that infuses all the different parts of our lives with alternatives to a culture of incarceration. Such a culture will nurture and sustain our struggle and provide space for political education, dialogue, and debate about what we are doing and what we need to do.

In order to figure out why people get locked up and under what circumstances, we need to examine what gets identified as root causes — a tactic that requires us to look at the competing priorities of the systems in which we live and understand why they work well for some and horribly for others. The systems of race, class, gender, and sexuality, for instance, are commonly understood to allow some people's needs and ideals to be privileged over others. They are constantly in flux and rely heavily upon each other for meanings. By exploring why and how those systems work for some and not for others, we can learn to counter their negative effects on those people who are most often put in cages.

To address strategies for opposing the PIC, activists must engage on both theoretical and practical levels. Contemporary struggles for justice and liberation are taking place on an entirely different terrain than the one faced by the activists of the '60s and '70s. We cannot engage in single-issue struggles, because all the issues intersect. What does social change look like in the era of globalization? How do these conditions affect and influence our strategies for social, political, and economic power? The voices of today's radical activists, particularly

ANOTHER **VOICE**

The more lawless our government becomes, the more it stresses and prosecutes law-breaking on the part of its citizens, and the more it builds jails and prisons, and the more it imprisons and for longer and longer periods of time.

— Elizabeth McAlister

activists of color, are sorely missing from the theoretical debate. Those who are most affected by the system should chart the direction for creating its demise.

Organizing against the PIC is as much about building something for people as it is about fighting something that is destroying people and communities. Further, it is an ongoing effort to create alternatives, not only to incarceration but also to the culture of punishment we're all but completely accustomed to.

REFERENCES

Churchill, Ward, and Jim Vander Wall. *Agents of Repression: The FBI's Secret Wars Against the Black Panther Party and the American Indian Movement.* South End Press, 1988.

Dyer, Joel. *The Perpetual Prisoner Machine: How America Profits from Crime.* Westview Press, 2000.

Gilmore, Ruth Wilson. *Golden Gulag.* University of California Press, 2000.

———. 1999. "'You have dislodged a boulder': Mothers and Prisoners in the Post Keynesian California Landscape." *Transforming Anthropology* 8(1 and 2), (1999), pp.12-38.

Holt, Thomas. *The Problem of Race in the Twenty-First Century.* Harvard University Press, 2000.

Jones, Charles E., ed. *The Black Panther Party Reconsidered.* Black Classic Press, 1998.

Prisonactivist.org. "Women in Prison" [online]. www.prisonactivist.org/women-in-prison.html, [date unknown].

Smith, Neil. *The New Urban Frontier.* Routledge, 1996.

Torres, Andres, and Jose Velazquez, eds. *The Puerto Rican Movement: Voices from the Diaspora.* Temple University Press, 1998.

▶ 20.

Activating Youth in Marginalized Communities
Youth Peace

| ASUF ULLAH |

In New York City, there are seven communities that make up 90 percent of the prison population in the state. It's no coincidence that those seven communities are also the most marginalized, the most drug infested, and the most gun infested. The key to creating serious change in these and other marginalized communities is to get young people of color involved in the activist movement.

Youth Peace (YP), a youth-run program of the War Resisters' League, works to counter militarism and the culture of violence it perpetuates. Currently, we're extending our analysis of militarism to include looking at the expansion of the prison industry, over-incarceration, and the targeting of young people. Our goal is to simplify complex issues that are not easily understood and to provide resources, tools, and information to young people.

One of our projects is called AWOL — a magazine and hip-hop CD made in collaboration with the Central Committee for Conscientious Objectors. AWOL's goal is to reach out to communities and raise the consciousness of people who often feel disenfranchised from the activist agenda. Many young people on the streets just don't speak the activist language. And more often than not, activism doesn't speak the language of poor young people of color. Hip-hop is our bridge. It's the language of the hood, of young people who are directly affected by the issues we're struggling with.

We also created a comic strip series for the magazine called *Make It Plain* — an expression that Malcolm X would use whenever he spoke about issues. It's how he broke down issues, so they would be accessible to people who don't understand a lot of the esoteric jargon in activist circles. We explain terms like WTO, Prison Industrial Complex, IMF — things that aren't necessarily understood by the communities that are most targeted by those issues.

A lot of the interest in YP stems from young people who feel disenfranchised by the constant military presence in their schools or communities. Young people call us up and want to know how to get out of the delayed entry program they signed up for or how they can get out of the military once they're in. We organize against military recruitment on and off campuses — particularly in marginalized communities, where young people are prey for the military who pander to their needs for insurance, education, and so on. One of our tools is a video called "It's Not Just a Job," which offers an alternative analysis and perspective of the military.

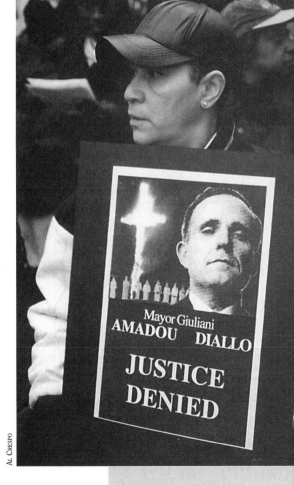

AL CRESPO

Mayor Giuliani
AMADOU DIALLO
JUSTICE DENIED

Recently, we organized a hip-hop show and screened the film "Lockdown USA." We expected maybe 10 or 20 people to show up. Not only was the theater packed, but we also had to turn people away. We'd organized a panel discussion, but instead everyone just wanted to talk. (This was right around the time that four New York City police officers were acquitted of all charges for the brutal murder of Amadou Diallo, a West African immigrant who was shot 41 times. The verdict clearly showed how blatant racism is and how the system just doesn't work for people of color.) As we'd hoped, the event definitely activated young people who weren't involved yet in activist circles.

▼

Asuf Ullah lives in New York City. He is a longtime peace activist and coordinator of youth programs.

LINKS

www.nonviolence.org/wrl/y-
index.htm

▶ 21.

Giving Back
Supporting Youth Movements of Resistance for Educational Equity

| LUIS SÁNCHEZ |

I am a perfect example of globalization. My parents left Mexico because they couldn't find a job or any opportunities there. They were part of a whole labor pool that continues to migrate from small towns in Mexico to work in the United States. So, I've witnessed and felt what it's like to be part of a group of people (especially young people of color) who've been attacked by laws that limit or deny them access to health care, schools, and public institutions because they are undocumented immigrants.

As a teenager, my community was 99.9 percent Latino. It was all I knew. Growing up, we just stayed in our community, because the bus routes were set up to keep people in their own areas. It's still virtually impossible to get to the West Side of Los Angeles by bus. You can get to the East Side, but not the other way around. When you grow up in that kind of environment, you begin to understand who has power and who doesn't and how racism, sexism, and classism are used to keep people in their place.

After high school, I was accepted to UC Berkeley. I was very fortunate, particularly when you consider that for every Latino male who is in college, four are in the prison system. While I was in

▲
Luis Sánchez

college, I had to keep asking myself: What am I going to do with my education? Am I going to take advantage of my luck and privilege and not care about where I came from, not care about social justice? Or am I going to do something to change things?

After I graduated, I decided to go back to East LA and work on the issues in my own community. I figured: So what if I don't make as much money as I could be if I was doing other things, as long as I can make enough to live and be happy. Which I am.

To me, educational justice is the key issue at the center of everything. The way the system works now for young people of color, especially those from inner-city communities, is it tracks them into a remedial and non-challenging education. Teachers don't teach these students to develop a critical analysis, and if you don't develop a critical analysis, it's much harder to understand the way power and racism work. Also, if young people do think and criticize the system, they're marginalized. So what they're producing are young people who don't think and won't criticize; who will just be sucked into low wage or nonunion jobs or be roaming the streets, where they can easily become part of the prison industrial complex.

The way I see it, schools are really just preparing kids for the culture they're going to live in. High schools are becoming like police states, located in gated compounds. They're getting them used to having police around them 24/7. They're getting them used to being in jail. In Oakland, they just passed a law where they're actually going to put police stations with jails on high school campuses. That's crazy! They don't need police stations — they need art programs, public space, and after-school programs.

People have been so dumbed down, they don't even realize what's happening. We have a nation of people whose jobs are leaving the country, where welfare's being cut, where schools are overcrowded, where laws are much more oppressive for youth, where there hasn't been a college built in the State of California since 1983, but where 21 prisons have been built. Just understand what that means: you have to fill these prisons up with people. Instead of dealing with real issues and creating more programs that allow for change, the prison industrial complex and the military industrial complex are being heavily funded. It's a system where the only options young people have are prisons, the armed forces, or low-wage/non-union jobs.

Like, within suburban schools, the way it works is that a lot of people of color are tracked within the framework around race and class lines. But within inner city schools — where the majority of the students are low income people of color — the whole school is tracked. For example, Roosevelt High School in Los Angeles has 5,500 kids: that's a small city. They're totally overcrowded, and they have the most sophisticated ROTC program in the nation, which translates as: Well, they're not going to succeed, because they really don't have any opportunity, so we'll just put the Army in there and tell them it's their only option.

On top of that, the Army lies to these kids. They say there's a guarantee they'll get money to go to college if they join the Army, which is the biggest farce. This country has made millions of dollars off that program. This whole belief that you're fighting for your country, this whole direction of promoting violence — that's the biggest hypocrisy. Young people are told to be nonviolent, not to bring guns to school, but at the same time there's an ROTC program that teaches young people how to march with guns. That's completely crazy.

Another problem is that there aren't enough resources in the schools for the whole student body, which means that at least one-third of the kids will not be given the resources necessary to graduate. I was a teacher; I know. You're given a class with 40 or 50 kids, where you don't have books until the fourth week, and even then you don't get enough books for all the students. Most of the work is on ditto sheets, which is basically just busy work instead of student-centered, project-based work where kids really get challenged. And then teachers take that on and say: Well, these kids are not going to succeed anyway, so why even teach them? They just expect kids to fail.

And when young people do start asking questions, when they begin to organize like they are now and ask these questions around race, gender, class, and sexuality, the establishment reacts and says: Oh, those people are too revolutionary.

I would never have thought that the three high schools in the neighborhood I grew up in would walk out to protest the school system, or that we would have a Youth Organizing Communities (YOC). I could never have imagined that I would be organizing in cities that I grew up in — but it's happened. It's all happening. And the reason is because young people are being proactive instead of reacting negatively toward the problems that exist in our communities. It just goes to show how all that energy can be channeled if you give them an alternative, not only to get involved in the community, but also to

ANOTHER **VOICE**

When you start finding out stuff, you stop being confined to your own little world, like: Oh, what am I going to wear tomorrow? What movie am I gonna see this week? You just get out of that whole zone of conformist life and actually open up your eyes. Because things are going on and its your responsibility to go out and do something.

— Sommer Garza

ask each other: Do you want to change the shit that's basically making it harder for you? Do you want your younger brothers and sisters or your kids to grow up in an environment like this? Do you want them to go to these kinds of schools? And they begin to see the bigger picture: it's not only about them; it's about their families, their younger brothers and sisters, their cousins, their kids. Then their actions become a lifelong vision, as opposed to a phase.

▼

Luis Sánchez grew up in Montebello, California, where he worked with refugees and young people organizing after-school programs and soup kitchens. He is a community organizer with Youth Organizing Communities and Inner City Struggle in Los Angeles.

⊟ L I N K S

www.schoolsnotjails.com

▶ 22.

Hell'a Story

A Lesbiana Warrior's Journey from Oppression to Liberation

| MALACHI LARABEE-GARZA |

Malachi Larabee-Garza

MALACHI

My mother's from Mexico City; my father's from Minnesota. I was raised in the Federal District in Mexico as a missionary until I was seven years old. Our mission was in the garbage dumps outside of Mexico City, where people live in cardboard shacks.

Seeing such a harsh reality really young and seeing the disparities between what reality is like in Mexico and what reality is like in the United States, and knowing that they both suck, influenced me to become an activist. It's easy to say: Oh, stuff is whack, you know, *over there*. People are suffering *over there*. But then to come back and be like: Wow, we're on welfare in the United States — that's really hard, you know? There's a lot of drug use in our communities. There's a lot of poverty in my community, and it doesn't go away even if you live in the American dream.

I believe I was raised with a consciousness that people were suffering. For me (for a while) and for my family, the answer was to give them a tract and tell them Jesus will make their life better. It was never a question that things were unfair, that people were hurting. It was that you could do something about it, and it was righteous and holy to do something about it — a high calling to do that work. But as my politics transformed, I kind of thought: Maybe this tract isn't going to help them eat tomorrow.

Around that time I came out as queer, as a lesbiana, and all of a sudden the church wasn't too happy with me. And my family wasn't too happy with me; I wasn't righteous any more. I wasn't doing the lord's work any more. And I was like: Maybe my path needs to be slightly different.

One morning my mother came to me and said, "Mija, in my morning prayer session our lord Jesus Christ told me that you think you're a lesbian and you're believing lies from the devil." And she opened a bible and told me 101 reasons why I was going to hell. They're really big in the idea that if you can pray hard enough, you can convert anyone.

At high school, I went from honor student to dropout, because I wanted to live and physically rock my appearance how I wanted and how I felt comfortable. So I cut off my hair and I was like: This is who I am. But there was no protection at my school. I was assaulted at my campus and all kinds of stuff. In class, when you're trying to learn about algebra and somebody behind you is saying you fuck your mother, or when "You're a faggot" is written on the chalkboard and the teacher doesn't erase it but does the math problems around it, well you stop being able to learn. You stop going to school.

I saw my reality crumbling. I saw my family life and my school life — the strongest things in the world to me — just crumble. I saw friends leaving and I felt unsafe. I realized that if I wasn't fighting back, then I was accepting a reality that was given to me by a system that I thought was wrong.

So I started to fight back. I started to get my feet on the ground. I started to say: This is not okay, and I began to love myself again. On campus I tried to start a gay/straight alliance, which is like a campus club that a lot of youth are now doing. It was hard. I put up posters at night, and the next day all our posters were ripped down. And there were posters that replaced them that said, "If you want to start a gay-bashing club, call this number." And there were pornographic drawings on the poster. The police came on campus, and I was told it was my fault and I was too obvious and I was causing trouble and who needs clubs?

My parents sent me to psychotherapists and psychiatrists and ex-gay changers. They actually have these weekend homes and retreats, and parents give up custody of their kids when they go there for a weekend, or for however long. So I ran away from one of those homes and went to San Francisco. I thought: Okay I'm gay — whatever. I'm a queer youth; I'll go to San Francisco and .... I pictured a white gay man handing me an apple and saying: Let me help you; you're one of us — it's a community. But instead, it was trying to get 25 cents out of people who spent $40 on lunch. It was no different.

So I went back to Pittsburgh and hooked up with a woman named Marie Blaze. She was a friend of the family, a lesbian who my parents thought they could convert. I didn't know this at the time; I just thought she was a really great person. Marie ended up taking me in and teaching me. I had stopped believing in love, because what I had been told was there was godly love, spiritual love, and also the undying love from parents — from mothers to daughters. And it was gone. But Marie helped me to believe in love again. She ended up taking in seven or eight queer youth off the street. She opened up her home. She sacrificed her materials, her free time. She sacrificed so many things that she could have done in her life — for us.

Marie always said she wasn't an activist. Yet I learned my activism style from her, because she was real. She wouldn't be out screaming and carrying a sign somewhere, but if I was in trouble at my school, if I said somebody gave me a bad look today, or my locker had pictures on it today, she was there in three minutes. If I said I had talked to my mother and she hung up the phone on me, she was there. Marie made me believe that it's about personal healing and personal liberation of your own situations and of your own mind. She really worked on my own heart and my own pain and always pushed me to stand up for myself. Through that I became more active on campus.

I was still pissed off about what happened at my original high school, so I kept fighting there and threatened the district with a lawsuit. I went to my principal and said, "I have the backing of the ACLU [American Civil Liberties Union] and this is the number of the law we're going to sue you with, and they're gonna whip your ass." And of course I didn't. I just knew that the ACLU existed. They got scared and started working with me. After that, I did call the ACLU and said, "Oh, I hope you're not mad."

I told the school that I had demands, and I wouldn't sue them if they were met. One was mandatory hate crimes tracking; one was starting a gay/straight alliance. I also demanded a staff development training once a year around queer youth issues. It was a very successful campaign. Now, the teachers in that school are a lot more conscious, and they have one of the biggest gay/straight alliances in all of Contra Costa County.

I was able to get an equivalent high school diploma from a continuation school and started organizing a little bit with the ACLU.

We put on a student rights conference — freedom of speech type stuff. That's when I started to realize that there were people actively fighting and that I could get involved. I felt I would be valued as a fighter, as somebody with knowledge.

I worked with the Pacific Center in Berkeley. It's a whole queer community center, and they do elderly stuff; youth stuff; HIV stuff; they do women's circles, and they have a speakers' bureau. I started going into high schools; started going into colleges; started going into treatment centers for youth and talking about my story. And it was becoming a story of liberation and not oppression. And I heard that through my own words.

It was becoming a really powerful process. Seeing how much you can touch people when you just come from your heart and you just say: This is what happened to me, and I know shit like this happens to you. And you can come beyond it, and you can struggle. I've had mothers bawling, saying I never knew.... And I've had youth crying and asking me to help them. I've had elementary school kids say: It's okay to be gay, I guess. I've been really blessed by doing that speakers' bureau.

One day I realized that people could do activism for a living. That blew my mind! I was like: Wait, I could help people; I could tell my story and I could make enough to have a place to live? I was working at a pizzeria when I saw the job advertisement for Just Act. They were looking for a campus organizer; someone who was young, from a diverse background, that had good public speaking and facilitation skills.

I go through a lot of different pain, but I'm coming to a place where I'm incorporating love, and what happened to me, and people's personal stories. Now it's having the privilege to work at a nonprofit and to spend my time thinking about the intricate connections between local and global issues.

I don't tell people: You need to be mad at Chevron; or you need to be mad at Shell; or you need to be mad at whoever — to me that's not my work. My work is: Where do you come from? You live in east Oakland? What are some conditions around you being poor? Oh, yeah — your drinking water. You can't drink your water. Is that a coincidence? How is your health? Oh, your mother has cancer; oh, she's 28! She has cancer and you live in east Oakland. Is that a coincidence? What's happening to your drinking water? What's getting dumped into your drinking water? It's about making connections and realizing that you do give a fuck about Chevron, because they're polluting your drinking water and that's why your mother has cancer. And that's about being poor. And that's about a system, you know?

So I see all of my activism as a responsibility, if nothing else, to where I've come from, and doing this work so another youth won't have to go through what I went through. Whenever I go back into a high school, I tell teachers: I want you to hear this story so when this happens you'll know what not to do.

And I know that believing in love again is a more powerful experience than any protest I've been in — on the real. More powerful than going and giving a speech somewhere and people applauding and standing up and it's thunderous. I really believe that if we can go to people and if they can really understand and feel these deeper things, then the rest falls in place.

▼

Malachi Larabee-Garza lives in Oakland, where she is a fierce youth organizer using art, culture, and popular education. Raised in a working class city, West Pittsburg, California, this mixed-race, Mexican-Irish self-proclaimed butch believes in strong community, faith, family, and the need for a revolution.

▶ 23.

21st Century Youth Leadership Movement

Fostering Community-Based Activism

| MEMBERS OF 21CYLM |

▲
21CYLM group

The 21st Century Youth Leadership Movement is a strong foundation of education and motivation to help nurture youth to their true liberation. Like a mother, it is a place of unconditional love. It is like a free world, where you come to explore yourself, your culture, and the dynamics of your community. It gives youth a chance to have their hands in the things that govern their communities and that ultimately govern their lives and the development of their people. It's an educational experience in learning how Black people in particular have had to struggle for their liberation and freedom through all facets of degradation and injustice.

What we do is go out into our communities and organize, connect, and develop young leaders, in and out of school. Young people come together in our trainings and camps to discuss different perspectives on what we see going on in our communities. It is very important to us that young people of all ages feel they can come to 21st Century as they are, whoever they are, to learn to be skilled, community-focused leaders who will resiliently and creatively take responsibility for themselves, their families, and their communities.

At 21st Century, we don't just come as organizers; we don't just come as people who live in Wilcox County or New Orleans; we bring our full selves to the movement. One of us can be a Christian and another a Muslim, and we don't have to change each other. We come as activists, organizers, physical and spiritual beings able to bring all of ourselves into a space where we are respected. This gives us an opportunity to be unified, and in that unity so many things can be accomplished.

The elders in our program ask us: What is it about 21C? Is it the skills training program; is it the 1,2,3s of organizing that keep you coming back? And we tell them: No, we come to experience what it's like to be in the world the way it should be all the time – a world that allows us to have a true vision about what we're working toward. For example, if we get in an argument, another person will come and mediate or pray or sing with us to make sure that the hurt gets healed right then and there. So often in this world, we don't have these kinds of opportunities that sustain us and allow us to grow.

In our workshops and camps, activists from the civil rights movement pass down their knowledge and experience in order to create a new cadre of leaders. Youth are able to learn from their mistakes and their triumphs. We talk about what happened to the Black Panther Party, what happened to people's movements. We talk about how you have to be resilient and creative and keep fighting for what you know is right. We share about the past and analyze the new movement from hip-hop and rap to the new strategies that support creating social change in our communities, in our world, and in our lifetimes.

One of our programs takes young people throughout the South to do an oral history project on people from the civil rights movement. The first requirement is to interview someone from the local community. At first, young people say: Hold on, we don't know people who were involved in the civil rights movement. And then they come back the next day saying: Oh, that was my mama, my grandmama, my

*Dakari Shabazz
and Antar Breaux*

aunt. This experience shows them the depth of pain that Black people have gone through and explains why some people don't want to say anything about the past. Having lived through those times, when people were thrown off bridges or hung, they don't want to pass on that kind of pain to their children. This is part of the reason why 21st C was created — in order to share that history, so that we would know what has gone on in the past, so that we will be prepared for the future.

Without a shadow of a doubt, if we want the world to be the way we envision it, there's no way racism can exist. And although there's no way that Black people can come together with any level of consciousness and not be aware of race issues, we don't have to teach about racism, not here, because we live it. As Black people, we don't really get together and say: OK let's talk about racism. It doesn't quite work like that with us. As Africans, we know racism exists, because we have felt the cold shoulders of it. But we do have to deal with the facts that we're being abused and exploited and we're human and we must be respected.

We do talk about reparations, and we know that no monetary token could repair what our African ancestors have gone through.

The majority of white Americans, white Europeans, won't acknowledge the pain that we've been through. They won't look at the facts; they won't explore; they won't watch a tape or sit down and go through the emotions of facing what their people have done to our people. Until everyone is educated about slavery, until people acknowledge that racism exists today, we will not move forward.

At 21st Century, many of us believe that in order for healing to take place Black folks need to be able to express their truth without fear of what's going to happen. When we start talking about slavery and race, blocks come up immediately in the white community. White people won't deal with the heaviness of the exploitation, the murder, the rape, the hangings and burning, because the denial is part of maintaining their own sanity.

White people have to deal with white privilege and apologize for the pain they have inflicted. Black people aren't sitting around saying: Oh I wish white folk would say 'I'm sorry.' It has to be about action and about sharing privilege. If there is a door you know somebody can't go through because they're a person of color, then make sure they can get through that door. The other major thing is checking folks. Some of the hardest work white folks are going to have to do is check other white people and say: Hold up. I heard you say what you said and saw you do what you did, and it's unacceptable.

As for the Black community — it's going to have to be unacceptable to us, too. We're going to have to make sure that we aren't hurt. I think the Black part of it only Black folk can do, and I think the white part of it only white folk can do. White folks cannot bring healing to our community; they cannot come forward and save us. It's impossible, but we can all save our own people.

J.L. Chestnut

▶ 24.

Getting the Truth Out Louder

The Civil Rights Movement

| J.L. CHESTNUT |

I was born in Selma, Alabama 70 years ago. My mama, who's 89, says that I'm almost as old as she is! Up until about three years ago my law office was only about four blocks from the house in which I was born. She was fond of coming by to tell me I hadn't gone very far. In 1958, when I came back here to practice law, only 150 black folk out of a pool of 30,000 were registered to vote. Each one of those people had to be vouched for by a white person. If some white person didn't say Ol' Ned was all right, then Ol' Ned didn't get registered.

Back then, there were black and white water fountains, black and white restrooms, and black women could not try on a dress or a pair of shoes in a downtown department store. No blacks had any jobs downtown anywhere in Alabama, except as drivers to the delivery people. No black had served on a jury anywhere in Alabama in 100 years. The police were a law unto themselves in the black community. They did whatever, whenever, to whomever. And you did not ask a question or they'd find your body floating in the Alabama River.

I've known black men to be killed for not saying 'Sir' to a white person or yielding the sidewalk to a white woman. Those were awful times. And I'm just talking about a few years ago — 1958. That's

| 114 |

the reason I came back. When you have been born into those circumstances and you have to live under that, it either makes you or breaks you.

I was the first black person to open a law office in Selma. With the help of the NAACP, I started arguing about the systematic exclusion of blacks from the jury. We finally won that fight. Then we started to argue about integrating the public schools. We were in the process of changing all these things when the Civil Rights movement exploded in the streets of Selma. I was one of the seven people who actually persuaded Martin King to come here.

The public does not know this, but Martin King did not initiate the demonstrations in Selma. We'd been in the streets two years before we persuaded him to come and join with us. John Lewis, Rap Brown, Julian Bond; a whole host of people; younger folk from SNCC (Student Nonviolent Coordinating Committee) had been here two years working with us, getting their heads whipped and getting killed before we got Martin to come. But once we got Martin here, that focused national attention on us. It also reached certain blacks who would not march unless someone like Martin asked them.

If Martin told me once he told me one hundred times, "They will keep coming back for us until not a one is left standing." And to some extent he was right about that. He always talked about his death

A wall in the Voting Rights Museum in Selma, Alabama features cards signed by people who participated in the historic Selma to Montgomery March in 1965.

and everybody else's because he knew his days were numbered. We all knew it. Those were dangerous times.

I don't think this generation fully understands how we got where we are. There is an assumption on the part of some people that things have always been this way. Oh, there might have been a few marches, years ago, but they don't know the extent of the blood, the suffering, the deaths. And that's not limited to young people. Professor Roger Wilkens says, "We blacks and progressive whites have never fully told the story of racism to white America. If we could ever really tell it in all its horror, how it undermines the very core of this nation, and how it holds everybody back, then there would be a different response from white America," and I think he's right. On the other hand, I don't feel that this generation of young people are just lost; there are young people out there now who are every bit as dedicated to the cause as we were 40 years ago.

People tend to think that in the 1960s, there was great unity in the black community and everybody was out marching, sacrificing, and protesting. Nothing could be further from the truth. It was a handful of us. Those numbers magnified later on, but even then nothing like 30 million blacks were out demonstrating. It does not take some immense army to forge forward when you're operating in terms of truth and justice. Surely, I would like to see many, many more young people involved, but I understand that Christ only had 12 disciples and one of them was a traitor. I think that my generation, the twilight generation, has to spend more time teaching and otherwise communicating the true history. Not to just young blacks but to young people, period.

When I talk to young folk about the high standard of living that we enjoy in this country, I tell them: I'm not sure that it's a bargain when you really consider the price, which includes 350 years of slavery and another 100 years of near-slavery. It includes a foreign policy that has reduced Central and South America to some sort of serfdom for this country. The price we pay for this standard of living, I would be willing to forgo; I suspect that more Americans, if they knew what it costs, would also be willing.

Once again, it seems to me that everything gets back to trying to get the truth out louder. We have to keep struggling and communicating. We have to be willing to be called troublemakers. Things are not all that hopeless. They're difficult, they're complicated, but we just need to keep pushing forward. We need to tell the truth; we need to live the truth; we need to be the truth. And I don't have any doubt in me, that will change the world.

▼

J.L. Chestnut is the founder of the Federation of Southern Cooperatives and author of Black in Selma: The Uncommon Life of J.L. Chestnut, Jr.: Politics and Power in a Small American City.

▶ 25.

No Picnic

A Campaign Against Environmental Racism

| TERRI SWEARINGEN |

ROBERT C. VISSER, GREENPEACE

▲

Terri Swearingen

I first learned about Waste Technologies Industries (WTI) in 1982. Owned by a multinational Swiss corporation (Von Roll), WTI is located in the flood plain, immediately on the bank of the Ohio River in an impoverished minority Appalachian river town. It operates in a residential neighborhood, where the closest home is only 320 feet (97 meters) away, and the smoke stack is level with the front doors and windows of a 400-student elementary school that's 1,100 feet (335 meters) away on a bluff above the site.

The WTI case is a story about our society. We've learned that the agencies set up to protect public health and the environment only do so if it's non-threatening to corporations. We have struggled to protect the health and welfare of our children, only to experience our own government subverting our democratic system — providing ways for the corporations or money men to get around the law.

It took a decade for us to learn that working within the system didn't benefit the people. We pursued legal, political, and economic strategies in trying to protect our children, with little effect. In 1991, we decided to step up our direct action campaign. When our own government was not obeying the law, we had to break the law to force the issue.

Our first act of civil disobedience resulted in arrest, following a rally attended by 1,500 citizens. Thirty-three citizens, including actor Martin Sheen, climbed the fence surrounding WTI. We were thrown in jail for three days.

The next month, when Ohio Governor Voinovich refused repeated attempts to meet with us and continued to defend WTI, we went to his mansion and posted "For Sale" signs on his lawn. By accident, we caught the governor as he jumped into a waiting car, and we asked to speak with him. He responded by saying, "I'm not going to talk with you. I have nothing to say." When reporters asked for comments, without thinking, I called the Governor a 'weenie,' saying he lacked the guts to face his constituents.

To my embarrassment, the quote not only appeared in the next day's paper, but they had highlighted it. So we decided to have some fun with it. We used a hot dog to symbolize Governor Voinovich being a 'weenie on waste.' Within three weeks, we were back at the Governor's mansion holding a 'weenie roast' in front of his home. I got to be the 'weenie Governor,' dressed in a hot dog costume and a mask of Governor Voinovich. I can't remember the exact words, but the speech went something like this: *Frankly*, I don't *relish* the *pickle* I'm in. I need to *mustard* the courage to *ketchup* with front-end

Terri Swearingen is an activist, a registered nurse, and a mother. She lives with her family in the Ohio River Valley, where she cofounded the Tri-State Environmental Council, and has worked for over 12 years in an effort to stop the construction and operation of one of the world's largest commercial toxic waste incinerators.

prevention. I feel like a *weenie* being squeezed between both sides of the *bun*: one side represents citizens who don't want to be poisoned, and the other side's the polluter, who wants the profit. It's no *picnic* being in this position. I'm gonna get *roasted*.

We got a lot of media attention. We got our message out and we had fun doing it. We kept up the weenie campaign for over a year. At the time, we were making regular trips to Columbus, and we never failed to deliver the Governor a hot dog from one of the street vendors. When we weren't in Columbus, citizens made sure he got the message by mailing him jars of those teeny cocktail wieners. We had pressure-sensitive stickers made with the Governor's phone number on it and a picture of a hot dog. The sticker said, "If you think the Governor is a 'weenie on waste' call him." We put the stickers on packages of hot dogs and buns throughout Columbus grocery stores.

In an ongoing, relentless, momentum-building campaign, involving direct action and civil disobedience, we were able to escalate the WTI issue to the national level and cause federal policy changes. We haven't stopped WTI yet, but we motivated Congress to conduct its first-ever hearing to look at the ways the EPA bent the rules to help industries they are supposed to regulate. We prompted a nationwide freeze on the construction of new toxic waste incinerators and forced an overhaul of federal combustion regulations. We compelled the federal government to acknowledge the serious risk that pollution poses to the food chain. Citizens working to stop WTI have been credited with being the driving force behind EPA's action to implement national siting standards for hazardous waste management facilities.

I feel strongly that civic involvement is a responsibility and an important part of maintaining democracy. We have to grow to become a stronger force. We have to be more effective organizers. And we have to have fun doing it.

▶ 26.

Crisis in Ogoniland
The Price Paid for Oil

| OWENS WIWA |

The Ogoni people are a small ethnic group in the Niger delta of Nigeria. The population is 500,000 in a 404-square-mile (975-square-kilometer) area. Within this area there are 100 oil wells; Royal Dutch Shell drills 98 wells and Chevron, 2.

Shell oil started drilling oil in Ogoni in 1958, Chevron in 1973. In 35 years, they have drilled over 900 million barrels of crude oil, which is estimated at about $30 billion. Shell states that only about 646 million barrels have been extracted. One wonders if difference between our figures (calculated from their books) and theirs represents the amount of oil spilled. Associated with the extraction of this oil have been severe environmental destruction of the area and health risks to the people.

Shell uses bad processes and procedures (which they will not use in the West) to drill the oil — we refer to this as an example of environmental racism. They flare-off a lot of gas horizontally, very close to human habitation. This lets out poisonous gases into the atmosphere, which the people breathe in, and creates a constant experience of 'daylight' for the people who live nearby. As the oil is extracted, a lot of it spills out onto farmland and seeps into the drinking water. These spills smother the land with oil, kill masses of fish and other aquatic life, and

Owens Wiwa

introduce devastating acid rain. Fishermen and farmers are despondent because Shell does not clean up after the spillage, and that means people's livelihoods and health are seriously affected.

So, in the 1990s, the people decided to complain and mobilize themselves. Three hundred thousand people came out to the streets to demonstrate against the environmental racism of Shell. Shell responded by arming the soldiers and policemen. They actually brought arms into the country and gave money to the soldiers, who started to abuse the rights of the people.

My brother Ken Saro-Wiwa and all of our colleagues who headed the movement were very vocal, complaining about the environmental destruction and the human rights abuses. In 1994, four chiefs in our area — four prominent men — were killed in circumstances we believe were set up by the government. My brother and our colleagues were arrested and charged with murder, even though they were not even at the scene of the crime.

Immediately after Ken was abducted from his house, I went to all the police stations and talked to all my army friends in Port Harcourt, and none of them knew anything. I knew then that it was serious. I took the first flight from Port Harcourt to Lagos to see his lawyers and, whilst I was seeing them, it came on the radio that I was wanted for the murders, as well. Immediately, I went underground with my wife, who was also wanted. The search for us was very intensive. At one point, we were virtually staying in about three safe houses in a day.

While I was in hiding, I tried to have contact with people from the press, churches, embassies, human rights groups, and Amnesty International. I asked them to seek out and expose the truth and help free my brother and our colleagues. But to no avail. The fact that I wasn't successful in getting Ken released has affected me a lot, but I don't know what I could have done that I didn't do.

Three days after my brother and the others were hanged, we fled to Ghana, until it was not safe to be there either. Through the help of Anita Roddick and The Body Shop, we were able to get tickets to go to Britain. We boarded an aircraft that we didn't know was heading back to Nigeria for fuel. The police came onto the aircraft, but somehow I was lucky and they didn't recognize me or my wife. Later, we came to Canada as exiles.

Telling the story of our people is very important. We travel around and talk about the alliances between big corporations and dictatorships who try to subdue environmentalists. We share with people how, in Ogoni, the youth are one of the most active groups because the future belongs to them.

Actually, the women in Ogoni are the most powerful. They are very well organized, and they empowered us to speak out, because they were behind us. The women are on the front lines of the environmental movement. They are the farmers, and they see the effect of these oil spills and gas flares on their crops and their yields. They are the people who usually come to my clinic with the children whose lungs have been poisoned by gas fumes. They are also the people who, when their children are arrested, carry most of the pain. To me, these are the first people that need assistance — so that they can have more autonomy to speak out. My focus is on empowering these women. Once that is done, I think, from the perspective of being an activist from Nigeria, we'll have gone a long way.

At present, in Nigeria, we have a democratic government. That is a big change for us. Within democracy there is more freedom of speech, which we need. But structurally and institutionally there has not been a change in the way the corporations behave. They still use excessive force in Ogoni toward those who struggle against the abuses associated with the oil.

Although the United States condemned the government in Nigeria at that time, it is still one of the biggest consumers of Nigerian oil in the world. I want the youth in the US to realize what power they have to stop such atrocities. They can lobby the Congress to help raise awareness of human rights issues and to show how these abuses are linked to the corporations and the economy. Youth can also use their energy and their purchasing power as consumers to influence the decision of corporations. That is where we need their voices and their assistance.

Dr. Owens Wiwa is a medical doctor, human rights activist, and executive director of AFRIDA, the African Environmental and Human Development Agency. AFRIDA is a non-governmental organization committed to improving the quality of African communities in resource-bearing areas that are overrun with transnational mining companies.

LINKS

www.mosopcanada.org

▶ 27.

Por Vida

In Solidarity with the U'Wa People

| ABBY REYES |

▲

Abby Reyes

It's been two years now. In March 1999, my partner Terence Unity Freitas and two Native American colleagues were kidnapped and assassinated by left-wing guerrillas in northeastern Colombia while exiting U'wa indigenous land coveted by US oil giant Occidental Petroleum (Oxy). For almost a decade, the U'wa community has worked to protect their lives, culture, and ancestral territory from the next wave of imperialist colonization — that of energy resource exploitation by transnational corporations and the Colombian government. Terence, with indigenous rights workers Lahe'ena'e Gay and Ingrid Washinawatok, worked with the community's leadership to support and strengthen that struggle.

Just this afternoon, I finally opened Terence's boxes of photographs that he took during earlier trips to U'wa territory. An electric blue butterfly flutters gracefully out of the box. A waterfall taller than the sky plunges into a deep green pool, surrounded by misty forest. A young U'wa woman weaves the satchel that I now carry. An 87-year-old man rigs his bird trap with a smirk. Terence, led by children, sloshes through the mud and up a tree. A pair of parrots, zealously green. White egret. Scarlet ibis. Seeing life teeming and

| 125 |

U'wa woman and child

TERENCE UNITY FREITAS

thriving, vital, through the glimpses of these photos, I begin to breathe deeply again. The fear and burden of opening these boxes — building over these two years as Terence's close buddies and I continue to work in solidarity with the U'wa community — dissipates with the flap of a butterfly's wings.

There are other photos that offer silent testimony to an ecosystem jolted out of equilibrium. Bright yellow plastic buoys linked together across a stagnant pool of oil-soaked creek bed. Oil in the rocky wash. Armed soldiers jockeying out the side of a jeep. An Oxy helicopter trailing Terence's walkabout. An oil pipeline, carrying the blood of our mother pulsing through its artificial artery, winding to a port at the ocean's shore, where 60 percent of the oil travels straight to US refineries.

U'wa men and women, who have been chosen by their elders to represent the community to the outside world, speak from the depths about their spiritual mandate to protect the equilibrium of the Earth by protecting their own land *kajka-ika* — the heart of the world. Every summer, this mandate is instilled and strengthened throughout the community during purification through fasting and a recitation of their oral history that takes two weeks to sing.

Most knowledge is stored in song. At one recent meeting, Armando, the U'wa community's secretary of education, drew for us a map of seven headwaters in U'wa territory that are affected by Occidental's new oil project. Stuck, Armando sang and sang to recall the name of one of the rivers into which Oxy is dumping displaced mountainside. The U'wa are of that land and those waters. When the

U'wa people are displaced from that home, a millennium of knowledge about maintaining peace and equilibrium there are displaced, too. Displaced mountain clouds the clear flow of river.

In another series of photos, taken in 1998, Terence and two U'wa men stand upon sacred boulders overlooking the planned drill site. The site, called Gibraltar 1, is home to a couple of different U'wa communities and ritual grounds. It is also home to a number of non-U'wa *campesinos*, who are as opposed to the prospective oil exploitation as the U'wa themselves.

In late 1999, the Colombian government declared Gibraltar 1 to be outside of U'wa territory. Within weeks thereafter, it swiftly bypassed all pretense of community consultation — an internationally and constitutionally guaranteed right of indigenous Colombians — and issued Oxy it's license to drill. But before the government moved to kick the U'wa out of Gibraltar 1, the U'wa bought their ancestral land back from the *campesinos*. Through this unencumbered, legally titled purchase, the U'wa (in effect) bought parcels of the drill site itself — the land granted to Oxy on the basis of it being outside of U'wa territory. The Colombian courts are still trying to figure this one out.

In a move to ease the requirements to begin drilling, the Colombian government illegally changed the zoning of the U'wa land. A few days later, U'wa leaders presented the government with archival evidence of colonial titles for that land from 1661. These 14 "Royal Land Deeds," issued by the King of Spain, recognize preexisting rights of indigenous people in Colombia — claims that later Colombian laws uphold. When met with this documentation, the Colombian national ministers sat in silence. They had no reply. Their reply came implicitly two weeks later, when Colombia poured substantial military resources into protection as Occidental moved its equipment into place for drilling.

Absent from Terence's boxes are photos documenting the massive nonviolent mobilizations that the U'wa maintained for the months leading up to the start of the drilling. Terence didn't live long enough to see it. Swelling to over 4,000 people at its peak, the U'wa — along with farmers unions, students, clergy, other indigenous groups, and even local Oxy workers — mobilized for months at a time to occupy the drill site, block access roads, block national ministries in Bogotá and the Pan-American highway.

In Colombia, the U'wa struggle has become one of several symbols of resistance to the development model that pins its hopes on megaprojects like oil exploitation to provide economic panaceas. They are taking a stand for their vision of ecological and people-centered development. But the political climate of escalating armed violence has muted almost any international echo of this stand, despite a great show of solidarity through direct action and advocacy in the US and Europe.

Shortly after Terence, Ingrid, and Lahe' were assassinated, conservative members of the US Congress used the murders as a rallying cry for the US to quit its support of the peace talks in Colombia. Instead, our Congress has moved to shape and help implement the Colombian government's new military offensive. On March 30, 2000, U'wa leader Roberto Perez and I sat waiting for a delayed advocacy meeting with one US Congressional ally. In his office, we watched the TV monitor of the House floor count the votes leading to Plan Colombia's approval. Under the banner of the drug war, Plan Colombia ties extensive military aid directly to Colombia's willingness to open its petroleum resources to foreign corporations.

As such, Plan Colombia amplifies a movement that is swiftly changing the face of the agrarian landscape and provides perfect circumstances for an oil company to once again use the chaos of war to settle in as indigenous communities, such as the U'wa, are wiped off the map.

There is one image of Terence sitting cross-legged in the shade of a thatched porch awning, leaning up against the wall of a wooden house. The photo is taken from the side. The jungle teems with heat in the high sun beyond him, blackening his silhouette. He is 24. He is hunched slightly over a notebook. I imagine him pensive. I imagine him tired and full — full of stories to tell and life to give. As I look, I realize that this is the photo we used at his memorial service to accompany the text of a letter he wrote to a friend about working with the U'wa. In the letter, he first conveys despair about the civil war and cynicism about whether our work for peace will be able to make a dent. Then he goes on to describe a menarche ceremony, in which his U'wa companions allowed him to take part:

> Sometimes one would end and begin the
> song that the other was finishing .... Every
> once in a while, there would be silence,
> when the medicine people had all stopped
> their songs. Silence of voices but not of
> sound. The reverberation of hours and
> hours of singing stays in the house, in the
> wood, in the earthen floor. Then the singing starts
> again .... That is the reason we are
> doing this work, so that people can listen to singing.

COURTESY OF ABBY REYES

Terence Unity Freitas

It's been two years now. Terence's song, we know now, was a sweet, brief harmony to the Earth's timeless rhythms. Like an electric blue flap of the butterfly's wings. Gone in an instant and forever imprinted on the memory, beckoning the breath to breathe deeper.

Abby Reyes is a law student at UC Berkeley. She works with community-based environmental defense projects, including the U'Wa Defense Project in the US and the Environmental Legal Assistance Center in Palawan, Philippines. She is the cofounder of Women Working for Change, an international community of young women working for social and environmental justice.

LINKS

www.moles.org/uwa

▶ 28.

Globalization
The New Face of Imperialism

| JIA CHING CHEN |

"**G**lobalization," "neoliberalism," "development," "under-developed countries." When we look at these commonly used phrases closely, we can begin to read a story that is much older than their use: the over 500-year history of US imperialism. This is also the story of the growth of capitalism and the blood of exploitation and genocide that has been essential to that growth. When we talk about globalization, we are not talking about any truly new phenomena. When we look at who is getting hurt by globalization and who is benefiting from the Structural Adjustment Programs, multinationals, the WTO, the World Bank, and the IMF, we are not seeing anything new. When we talk about globalization, we are talking about the new face of imperialism.

To build a global movement for justice and against imperialist globalization, we must address oppression. Oppression is not 'an issue.' It is domination. It is a general shorthand term we can use to describe social systems — such as patriarchy, racism, heterosexism, and white supremacy — that create and institutionalize the privilege of one class of people at the expense of others. Oppression has historically gone hand in hand with exploitation,

▲

Jia Ching Chen

| 131 |

capitalism, and imperialism. Capitalism, which has never been separate from white supremacy or patriarchy, is an oppressive system. We can't dismantle imperialist globalization, corporate power, racism, sexism, or exploitation of people and the environment without addressing them all together.

THE HISTORY OF US IMPERIALISM

From their very first encounters with the indigenous peoples of the continent, Europeans began to oppress, enslave, and subjugate them.

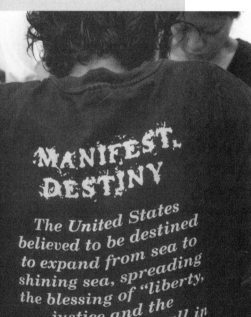

Christopher Columbus, reporting to the Royal Court, promised to them as much gold as they needed . . . and as many slaves as they asked for. He went on to say, "The eternal God, Our Lord, gives victory to those who follow His way over apparent impossibilities." Thus, oppression was sanctified by the Church from the beginning. The archdeacon presiding over the sale of the first Arawaks to arrive in Spain compared them to animals.

On the island of Haiti, where Columbus based his operations, in the first 2 years the Spaniards had murdered half of the indigenous population. In less than 60 years, Spain had enslaved, massacred, and worked to death millions of Arawaks living on the Caribbean islands. And by 1650, almost none of the original Arawaks or their descendents remained.

The empires grew on this model and its ideas. Soon the British arrived in North America and saw the land for their taking. In the name of the Church and in the name of progress, Manifest Destiny justified any atrocity for the material gain of the Empire and its colonists. These justifications rested on a base of racism, on distinctions that placed indigenous people in a subhuman category. By the time of the American Declaration of Independence, more than 90 percent of the indigenous people who were living in the colonized regions were murdered or dead from European diseases. This would soon be the fate of the rest of the continent's indigenous populations as well. The genocide brought about by imperialism throughout the Americas over the past 500 years easily exceeds 100 million deaths.

When the Indians and their land had been subdued, the capitalist need for expansion and rapid growth found many ways to sustain itself. Limitless cheap, expendable labor was central to this effort. The oppression of the Indians and the blindness to their genocide became easily applicable to the enslavement of Africans. The specific forms of that oppression continued to develop steadily, from the arrival of the first African slaves in 1619 to Jim Crow segregation laws to the racist death penalty and so-called justice system of today. By the time 50 million Africans had died in slavery or during the middle passage, only 4 million blacks were left to be freed in 1865.

The 200-year period from Columbus's invasion to the founding of the United States marked the beginning of the colonial era and the rise of the Western European empires. Imperialism created the means for the first mass accumulation of wealth that fueled the development of capitalism. This was the foundation for the United States. Imperialism and slavery not only provided the actual resources needed for the growth of the nation, but it also formed the worldview of our founding fathers and the ideas about foreign policy and spheres of influence that followed. With this understanding, we begin to see that the ideology of corporate globalization is a refinement of imperialism.

Global capitalism needed to exploit the resources and labor of the Third World in order to continue. However, resistance to colonialism grew and reached an international high point with the national liberation struggles and revolutionary movements of the past century. The Cold War grew out of the repression of these movements and their experimentation with socialism. The US integrated economic means of control and intervention into those countries where direct military occupation and political control became impossible.

By the 1960s, new methods of control were being developed to undermine revolutionary movements. The US supported brutal military governments and engineered coups. In collaboration with dictators and the Third World élite and with investment capital from private banks, the World Bank, and the International Monetary Fund, the US created huge debts and reestablished economic control over Third World countries.

Back home, Black Power and other grassroots movements grew in strength as oppressed people in the US struggled for democracy and their own liberation. The repression of resistance that the military waged abroad was brought home to Chicago, Oakland, New York City, and everywhere else in the country where people were organizing to make change. As in the Revolutionary War period, the hollow gestures of reform were more meant to pacify the anger and sense of injustice people felt than to address the roots of the problem of racism.

Today, institutions like the World Trade Organization and the Free Trade Area of the Americas continue to promote the profit and power interests of corporations above the concern for people, the environment, and justice. The disparity between poverty and wealth increases every year. Overwhelmingly, those who are getting hurt by the cutbacks in social services and jobs and by the increases in police brutality, prisons, and incarceration continue to be people of color. If we look, we can see that this is nothing new. We can see the roots of today's exploitation and oppression. If we look, we can see that the export of young women for sweatshop labor from Southeast Asia, the displacement of the U'wa in Colombia, the murder of the Ogonis and Ijaw in Nigeria for oil, the elimination of labor unions around the world, gentrification, and the mass incarceration of young people of color in the US all have a common history.

The movement needs to place fighting oppression at its center. We need to develop our concrete understanding of how oppression has grown hand in hand with capitalist exploitation over the past centuries. Until we create models for addressing oppression alongside the demands for alternatives and justice, we won't be able to succeed in our struggles. Young people have been educating about the history of oppression, while organizing for justice in their communities. Let us continue to learn and grow and lead.

Jia Ching Chen is an organizer with JustAct: Youth Action for Global Justice, in San Francisco. He works toward building unity and solidarity across race, class, and age lines by promoting participation and leadership of working class youth of color.

LINKS

www.justact.org

▶ 29.

Aloha 'Aina — Love the Land

The Struggle for Hawaiian Sovereignty

| 'ANELA 'O MAUNAKEA |

CARROLL COX, ENVIROWATCH

▲

'Anela 'O Maunakea

There are so many issues in Hawaii that affect my people, the future generations, and me. We are a colonized people — robbed of our language and traditions, our land stolen and used for its geopolitical, strategic, and military value instead of its sacred life-giving purpose.

In 1893, with the help of US Marines, our Queen Lili'uokalani was made a prisoner in her own palace by members of the white business community. Later, she was dethroned, the Hawaiian language was forbidden, our land was taken away, and disease killed my people by the thousands. In 1898, the Hawaiian Kingdom was annexed illegally to the US, and a false identity was forced upon us.

During my great-grandparents' time, they were made to feel ashamed to be Hawaiian. The stereotype was that Hawaiians were stupid and ignorant. They were forbidden to speak Hawaiian in school, and if they did they would be punished with a ruler to the knuckles, head, knees, or tongue. Before she died from cancer, my grandmother would tell us stories about how the missionaries used to invade our homes to make sure no one was speaking Hawaiian. Sometimes if she could hear her grandparents speaking Hawaiian with other elders, they would tell her: You hear nothing. Let it go through one ear and out the other.

My grandmother Yvonne was one of my greatest mentors. She practically raised me, which is traditional in the Hawaiian culture. It's because of her encouragement that I excel today, that I am politically and spiritually aware. She supported me when I fought to go to one of the first Hawaiian language immersion schools and when I fought the school system to give us the same respect and support they gave the English-speaking schools. Because of our fight, there are approximately 1,500 school children throughout the state of Hawaii who are taught in Hawaiian.

Today, I live on the island of O'ahu in the district called Wai'anae, which means 'the fresh water mullet.' It has the largest population of native Hawaiians on the planet: 60 percent of the more than 45,000 residents are native. We have beautiful beaches, rugged mountains, and spectacular valleys. A great abundance of food comes from both the ocean and the mountains. We have open sky, cool breezes, birds flying, dogs barking, pigs digging in the mud, freshwater springs, waterfalls, forests, and waves crashing on the coastline. The whole region is sacred to the Hawaiians.

Makua Valley, near where I live, is a beautiful valley untouched by development. There are numerous legends about it, hundreds of ancient sites (including temples and shrines), and over 30 endangered species. 'Makua' means 'parents' in Hawaiian. It is our church, our sanctuary, and our place of refuge. And for the past 60 years, the US Army has been bombing there.

During World War II, when martial law went into effect, the military condemned the valley, evicted the families who farmed and grew up there, and destroyed the community for target practice. Houses were bombed, the church was bombed, and the Army took over the lease for the cost of a single dollar. A measly dollar, in exchange for years of memories, history, legends, and tradition! At the time, the Army claimed that after the war, they would return the valley to its people. This has yet to happen. Today, the military is the second largest industry in Hawaii, and it occupies thirty percent of the Makua Valley.

Live fire has contaminated the Valley with unexploded ordnance and hazardous chemicals, and the people of Wai'anae — from newborns to elders — are at risk for the rarest to most common forms of cancer. In fact, the risk is amongst the highest in all Hawaii, and a lot of my own family has died from it. Two incomplete ground studies conducted in Makua found TNT, RDX, and HMX in the soil and chromium, lead, nickel, arsenic, PCB, and DNT in the waste treatment — all left over from explosives. Open Burn/Open Detonation sites were also confirmed to be contaminated by chemical waste from the Tripler Army Hospital nearby. The studies found chromium in a well, meaning that the water we drink is contaminated. This not only affects the native Hawaiian people but everyone who lives on this coast, as all the aquifers are connected.

We asked the Army to do an environment impact statement, an extensive study on everything from the soil to groundwater, but they didn't take us seriously and refused. We went to court and many people testified. The Army tried to dismiss the case, but the judge refused. I don't know how the people in the Army can sleep at night, knowing what's happening to us. They don't eat here; they don't hunt for food in our forest or waters. They don't fish here every day. Most of all, they don't live here. We do.

We don't need the Army; they need us. They train for war on our land and in the process destroy our heritage and culture. We want them gone. We are struggling for our self-determination. We are struggling for what is rightfully ours. I say stop training for war. Train for peace not oppression. Train for love not depression. Train for an identity; do not trample another's. Protect, don't endanger. Cherish, don't destroy. Our roots are in our tradition. Our identity lies with our struggles. Our culture is Aloha 'Aina — love the land. It is our birthright and the legacy of my people. My mother once told me, "We've waited for sovereignty for a hundred years. As sure as a Koa tree we can wait some more."

I try to educate as many youth as I can to be historically, politically, and spiritually aware. But this is not something I force on them; they have a choice to practice our traditions and speak our language — a privilege our elders never had. Many young people grasp the language easily; they understand the stories, our issues, but most of all our way of life. We teach them and they learn. As they understand, in turn they teach and reach out to others. They are now our hope and our future. I say to them, "Malama ka Waiolaa Kane. Malama ka Kai. Aloha 'Aina." Take care of the life-giving waters of Kane. Take care of the ocean. Love the land. I continue the legacy of my elders, and the youth will continue my legacy.

HONOR THE ANCESTORS

It is Hawaiian tradition to introduce our ancestors before ourselves. On my mother's side, my great-grandmother and great-grandfather are Katherine Duenas and Alexander Keolaokalani Maunakea. My

▼

'Anela 'O Maunakea is on the board of directors of Malama Makua (which means 'Cherish Parents'), a project for native sovereignty. Aside from her work with youth, 'Anela attends forums, conferences, and actions, bringing her knowledge of ancient Hawaiian chants and other traditional spiritual practices to the art of protesting.

grandma is Yvonne and my grandpas are Alexander Auna and Alexander Velles. My mother is Alexis Ku'uipo Kealani 'o Maunakea, a single, working mother of five children. She is a high school teacher of Hawaiian studies and Hawaiian language.

On my father's side, my great-grandmothers are Lucille Kealoha-Ka'ai'ai-Pa'ao'ao and Mary Kuluwaimaka and my great-grandfathers are Slomon Napulo'u and Juan Lopez, Sr. My grandmother is Nora Kuluwaimaka, and my grandfather is Juan Lopez, Jr. My father is Jesse Lopez, Jr., who has remarried and is a school bus driver.

Who am I? Maybe the question should be To Whom Am I? I am a tree that yearns for water. I am a cloud that has no rain. I am the daughter of *La*, the sun that shines fiercely. He teaches me to be a warrior, to have courage with a flame that burns. I am *Makani*, the wind that uplifts your spirit. I am *Waiola*, the waters of life. I am *Papahanaumoku* or Earth Mother. I am the voice that you hear whispered in your ear. I am somebody. I am a *Kanaka Maoli*, a native Hawaiian.

My ancestors, my elders, my mother and father, my family, my friends, and the Earth are my roots. They ground me and keep me true. They teach me to stand tall. I am their hope.

▶ 30.

Aboriginal Sin

| LEONARD PELTIER |

We each begin in innocence.
We all become guilty.
In this life you find yourself guilty of being who you are.
Being yourself, that's Aboriginal Sin, the worst sin of all.
That's a sin you'll never be forgiven for.

We Indians are all guilty, guilty of being ourselves.
We're taught that guilt from the day we're born.
We learn it well.

To each of my brothers and each of my sisters,
I say, be proud of that guilt.
You are guilty only of being innocent,
of being yourselves,
of being Indian,
of being human.

Your guilt
makes you
holy.

COURTESY OF THE PELTIER FAMILY

▲

*Cyrus (l) and Alex Peltier (r),
seen here with their
grandfather, work on
the Campaign to Free
Leonard Peltier*

THE INJUSTICE AGAINST LEONARD PELTIER

Traditional Native people have historically been opposed to leasing and selling Reservation lands for mining operations. In the early 1970s, members of the tribal government of Pine Ridge, South Dakota, headed by Richard Wilson and supported by the US government, favored the short-term benefits of uranium mining (despite the strong views of traditional people) and vehemently responded to anyone who opposed them.

On February 27, 1973 members of the American Indian Movement (AIM), together with many local Natives opposing the tribal government, began a 72-day occupation of Wounded Knee on the Pine Ridge Reservation. Their goal was to protest injustices against their tribes: treaty violations, repression against their people, and the intentions of others to mine their land. The United States government responded with a military-style assault against the protesters. Over a three-year period, more than 60 traditional Native people were murdered, and approximately 300 others were injured, several of whom were members of AIM.

In a historic shootout on June 26, 1975 two FBI agents and one Native man were killed. No investigation of the Native man's death ever took place, but three people were indicted for the deaths of the agents. Leonard Peltier was one of those indicted. Two were found innocent on the grounds of self-defense. Leonard Peltier (who

This **THANKSGIVING**
I wanted to thank you for:

- "Discovering" us
- Stealing our land
- Raping the women
- Killing us 'in the name of GOD
- Sharing with us your diseases
- Writing OUR history
- Taking us from our traditions
- Teaching us to be like you
- Giving me my name
- Poisoning our Mother Earth
- And, most importantly, celebrating this day!

▲

Emilio Guerrero

fled to Canada) was tried later in a different district by a different judge, after being illegally extradited from Canada. He was found guilty of first degree murder and sentenced to two consecutive life terms, in one of the most controversial trials of the century.

During the appeal process, previously withheld evidence pointed to Leonard Peltier's innocence. The prosecution admitted that they could not prove who had actually shot the FBI agents or what involvement Leonard Peltier may have had in their deaths. Nevertheless, Mr. Peltier remains in Leavenworth (Kansas) Federal Penitentiary. An embarrassment to the US justice system, Leonard Peltier has become a globally recognized symbol for the injustices practiced against Native peoples. There is an international outcry demanding his release.

LINKS

www.freepeltier.org

▶ 31.

No Borders

In Community with the Indigenous Peoples of Chiapas

| CYNTHIA P. MARENTES |

Sitting on a shelf as I walk into my living room, there is a photograph. Two little girls stand side by side, their eyes gazing into the distance, strands of sun-kissed hair lightly stroking their dresses, vibrant displays of color clinging to their thin, dark skin. Too shy to talk to me, I never knew their names, but I remember them and the faces of all the children I met on my two-week trip to Chiapas. Although we live miles apart from each other, the things that we share draw me closer to them. When I go through old pictures of my sister and me, I see those two little girls; when I talk to my nephew about his day in school or look into my son's big, beautiful eyes, the memory of those two little girls flows into my mind. My trip to Chiapas was brief, but the experience remains fresh within me to this day and probably will forever.

Cynthia P. Marentes

(far right)

FRANCISCO VAZQUEZ

The purpose of my journey was to assist two youth from Zapatista communities to produce a video on autonomous education. The project would show that the indigenous people in the villages of Chiapas were committed to the struggle of maintaining their identity, which included capturing their history, teaching younger generations their native languages, and establishing accountability among their own people for the education of their children.

Traveling into Mexico and then further into the rural areas of the state of Chiapas served to cement my views on the importance of preserving cultural identity and recognizing one's self-worth — not as an individual but as a vital organ of something much more significant: the community. It also helped me to know that I can still support Zapatista communities without actually living in them. Rather than letting the injustices of the world drag me along blinded for a lifetime, I can support indigenous rights and decelerate globalization within my own sphere of influence.

Injustice is not a word I take lightly. For me, it is a statement about the conditions that many around the world endure unnecessarily on a day-by-day basis. As a first generation, American-born daughter of Mexican parents — themselves organizers and fighters for farm workers' rights — I have known the injustices that corporations and government exert constantly on people from every corner of the planet. My trip to Chiapas

CYNTHIA P. MARENTES

▲

Niñas

showed me the wide reach and tight stranglehold of that injustice. Zapatista communities must deal with limited access to transportation, medicine, and nutritious food; no means of communication; a large military presence and that of other policing forces; constant harassment and intimidation; displacement; and worst of all, no recognition of their autonomy.

I journeyed into Chiapas with my parents' words in my mind: "The fight of one should be the struggle of the family and the cause of a community." These words have been deeply ingrained in my heart and into every second of my existence as far back as I can remember. My awareness of the struggle of farm workers along the US and Mexico border prepared me to understand the relationship between the Zapatistas cause for resistance and that of oppressed groups around the world.

What does a Zapatista farm worker in Chiapas have in common with a migrant farm worker in the US, after all? It is my belief that Zapatista communities and migrant farm workers in the US share a parallel existence. For one, both groups' survival is an everyday challenge that is punctuated by economic disparity, hazardous working and living conditions, poor health, malnutrition, and discrimination. Both are largely ignored and deemed throwaway societies.

Second, it is impossible for farm workers in general to subsist, much less support a family. That is true whether they live in Chiapas or the US. Crops produced through the slash and burn agriculture of the Zapatistas cannot compete with the production and harvesting methods of mega-corporations, who use biological engineering and liberal quantities of pesticides and enjoy immunity from environmental liability and taxation.

This idea was further illustrated to me when, on one day of shooting, our crew hiked into the highlands of a nearby Zapatista village. We prepared our equipment as a farmer began to clear his field of its old growth with nothing but a sharp machete. He could not explain specifically why he couldn't support his family off his small plot of land. But he knew that his situation was, in part, created by those who held political and economic power. He also told us why the struggle for autonomy was so important. He said that the belief and practice of the Zapatista communities is that all members work in collaboration with one another to ensure that their land is cultivated, that no one goes hungry (including those, such as teachers, who do not have time to work in the field), that their children learn how to work the land, and that their indigenous traditions endure. These are the very values that are being put at risk by globalization. I have also heard these concerns echoed across the US, particularly when it comes to migrant farm workers, a movement with which I am more familiar.

If you have come to help me you are wasting your time. But if you have come because your liberation is bound up with mine, then let us work together.

ABORIGINAL ACTIVIST SISTER

RICARDO LEVINS MORALES, NORTHLAND POSTER COLLECTIVE

Besides their problems with bureaucracy and funding limitations, Zapatista communities face the menace of military and paramilitary forces infiltrating their homelands and turning their everyday lives upside down. Similarly, farm workers in the US are

FRANCISCO VAZQUEZ

threatened by *contratistas* — farm labor contractors who exercise unchecked authority over the people they select for work in the fields.

The Chiapaneco communities face constant harassment, along with restrictions imposed upon them openly by the military and by their own neighbors. The roads are dotted with military checkpoints stationed strategically near entrances to Zapatista communities. The military presence has a profound effect on the lives of these people, as we saw on our first day of filming. Our crew was taping students singing the Zapatista hymn when, in the distance, we heard a military helicopter approaching. As the sound of the helicopter grew louder, the children's voices became softer, until they faded into a whisper. I also noticed the marginalization of Zapatista supporters within their own villages; neighbors, supporters of the ruling Mexican party, kept their distance from them and from us. The chasm that divided these two groups was very clear, despite the fact that the villages are small.

Farm workers in the border areas of El Paso, Ciudad Juarez, and Southern New Mexico also endure intimidation and threats. *Contratistas* steal the farm workers' daily earnings and gangs rob them while they sleep on the streets at night. And discrimination and marginalization are a fact of everyday life: farm workers are continually driven to one specific part of town by the dictates of influential organizations, such as the Downtown Business Association and tourism advocates from City Council.

In Mexico, the military patrols the Zapatista communities; in my hometown, policemen make their rounds telling homeless farm workers that they can only sleep in one specific block of town. And like the school children in the Zapatista community who became nearly silent when the sound of the military helicopter approached, US migrant farm workers have been silenced by enterprising groups and profit-hungry individuals who negate their importance in society and deny their contribution to our country's history.

Groups like the Chiapas Media Project, who work with indigenous communities and Sin Fronteras Organizing Project, who continue to assist migrant farm workers in the US are confronting the unjust realities of farm workers' lives. And their efforts are accomplishing noticeable change. Both organizations support youth who want to ease the struggle and dedicate their time to a worthwhile cause, and I have been fortunate to be a part of them. I believe that my relationship with Sin Fronteras continues to help many other organizations reach their goals.

The leaves on a tree are numerous and different, but the root binds them all together and gives them strength. It is for this very reason that I can turn to my picture of the two little girls from the Zapatista village and know that we are not so different. My struggle is theirs, and theirs is mine — regardless of distance, culture, age, or any other attribute.

▼

Cynthia P. Marentes resides in the border region of El Paso, Texas and Ciudad Juarez, Chihuahua, Mexico. She is a lifelong advocate of farm worker rights and fair labor wages and grew up as a member of the Marentes family – founders of Sin Fronteras Organizing Project. She spends as much time as possible with her son Benito.

LINKS

www.farmworkers.org
www.chiapasmediaproject.org

▶ 32.

A World in Which Many Worlds Fit
A Brief History of the Zapatista Movement

| JASON WALLACH |

The Zapatista uprising began publicly on January 1, 1994 — the day that the corporate globalizers and the governments that do their bidding put NAFTA into effect. Indigenous people representing 1,111 indigenous communities in Chiapas rose up and occupied five major cities and towns. Their demands sounded like the demands of many indigenous movements of the past: they wanted schools and teachers, clinics and doctors, land, and services such as electricity and running water. But they also wanted something more. Communities wanted to preserve their local traditions, languages, environment, and cultural values against poverty and forced dislocation. And they wanted to do it in a way that gave voice to the entire community, so that no one would ever feel left out of the decision-making process. The Zapatistas call this "creating a world in which many worlds fit."

Instead of listening to the demands of the people, the government responded with repression and violence. There were 12 days of gun fighting in the streets; a ceasefire was called when a massive protest in Mexico City demanded that the army and police back off from the indigenous communities. (Technically, the ceasefire

has held to this day. The Zapatistas have not fired a single shot.) The Mexican president sent in army troops and dislocated many people from their homes. Many were arrested; some are still being held in jail. Foreigners who wished to defend human rights or fight poverty through development projects were expelled from Mexico. Others went into hiding. The press was controlled and manipulated to tell the government's version of the story or simply remain silent. Paramilitary groups were formed, trained, and armed by officers who received their training from the US-sponsored School of the Americas (in Fort Benning, Georgia). These groups began a reign of terror by displacing thousands more from their homes.

The seven years between 1994 and 2001 have brought highs and lows — and every conceivable emotion — to the people of the rainforests and highlands of Chiapas. In February 1996, the government and the Zapatistas signed the San Andres Accords. The Accords allowed for indigenous communities to control their form of governance, maintain justice systems in accordance with indigenous law, and provide for education in native languages. It gave indigenous people part of what they were fighting for — control over their own communities. In a word: autonomy.

FRANCISCO VAZQUEZ

▲
Zapatista women filming

The Mexican government, under President Ernesto Zedillo, refused to implement what it had signed, however. Instead, Zedillo chose to pursue a strategy of civilian-targeted warfare that led to a massive militarization of Chiapaneco indigenous communities. Paramilitary squads (organized largely from unemployed youth in local pro-government towns) were trained by the army and state police. Journalists were targeted and pressured not to write about Chiapas. Hundreds of human rights activists from around the world were expelled from Mexico.

The Zapatistas cut off talks with the aggressive government in November 1996 but held steady and organized their communities autonomously. They withstood the militarization. They continued to make friends internationally and within Mexico, and they continued to demand the implementation of the San Andres Accords.

In 2001, a Zapatista caravan rode from Chiapas to the heart of Mexico City. They met tens of thousands of people along the way and eventually spoke in front of the Mexican Congress. Hope for the implementation of the Accords had never been greater. The Mexican Senate and Congress gutted the original bill, however, and passed one that denied the core guarantees agreed upon in the San Andres Accords: autonomy and democracy for indigenous communities. The National Indigenous Congress and the Zapatistas immediately rejected this bill, claiming that it represents a betrayal of the democratic will of the Mexican people by the Congress. As of this writing, people throughout the Americas are demanding the implementation of the San Andres Accords as a step toward justice in Chiapas.

LINKS

www.mexicosolidarity.org

▶ 33.

Turning Awareness into Action

Students for a Free Tibet

| LHADON TETHONG |

I n Tibet, there are now more Chinese than there are Tibetans. The Chinese government does not recognize the historical map of Tibet. Instead, they refer to the central region, one of three historical provinces, as the 'Tibetan Autonomous Region' (TAR). There, Tibetans are still a majority. And there, religious and political repression is at its worst.

People outside of Tibet seem to think that things are getting better, but in fact, things have been on the decline for the last decade. There was a period of relief in the '80s when Tibetans were given a little more freedom, at least compared to the dark days of the initial invasion/occupation and the Cultural Revolution. But now, the stories we're hearing by word of mouth from refugees and people escaping over the mountains are just insane. Even now, there are upward of 3,000 people a year escaping, most of them under the age of 18.

The Chinese are slowly wiping out Tibetan culture and tradition. From Tibetan Buddhist practices to language — everything is under threat of extinction, due to racist government policies. For example, strict monitoring groups enforce a two-child policy for Tibetan women, who can be forced to have an abortion, even into

COURTESY OF STUDENTS FOR A FREE TIBET

| 153 |

their ninth month of pregnancy. The groups monitor the women's monthly cycles. If she doesn't start menstruating, they find out if she's pregnant, and if she is, they give her two choices: abort the child or be fined. If a woman holds out and keeps her pregnancy until the ninth month, she is hounded and mentally abused. Women are terrified to go to the hospital, because they're afraid that they will be anesthetized, aborted, sterilized, and told that the baby died. Tibetans don't believe in taking life, so rather than face abortions, women often choose sterilization as a form of birth control. That's probably one of the ugliest and most serious issues happening inside Tibet today, and it's not just happening in isolated places — it's systemic.

The Chinese government's birth control policies in combination with forced resettlement (we call it population transfer) are colonialist. The government gives economic incentives — no-interest loans and land — to Han Chinese to move into Tibet; they then bring their families. Now, what is so disturbing is that if you're a Tibetan who renounces all your traditional practices, heritage, and family, then they will let you advance. You can even serve in the government and advance economically. But if you are a Tibetan who holds fast in any way to your religious or political beliefs for an independent Tibet, then you're targeted. This is the stuff we hear about most often.

Tibetans are imprisoned for speaking their mind or for refusing to attend a 're-education class,' where they are forced to denounce the Dalai Lama and basically spit on their own religion. The government says there's freedom of religion in Tibet, but we hear about students as young as seven who are having their protection cords (a Tibetan Buddhist practice) taken off their necks and burned in front of the class by their teachers. Tibetans also aren't allowed to learn their language; they have to learn in Chinese, in Mandarin. All of these efforts by the Chinese are assimilationist.

Our goal at Students for a Free Tibet (SFT) is independence for the Tibetan people. Our overall strategy is to turn awareness into action by raising consciousness and educating people through the different student chapters and student groups around the world. To meet our goal, we have been engaged in economic and political campaigning.

When the World Bank came up with a scheme in the summer of 2000 to loan China money (China is their biggest borrower) for projects in Tibet, we rallied all of our supporters worldwide and came out strongly against the loan — essentially to shame the World Bank. The loan was to build massive infrastructure projects that were contributing to the occupation and genocide of the Tibetan people. We were successful in stopping the World Bank. It was the first major victory of the Freedom Movement and a pivotal point. I think it changed our course and energized us. It showed everybody involved that we could actually affect things on an economic and political scale internationally.

We have been especially grateful for the official audiences that Students for a Free Tibet have had with the Dalai Lama. He's so keenly involved in international affairs and politics. He always starts out by expressing his gratitude for the work of students. He talks about how he believes that youth know what is best for the future and that they should teach older people how to do things properly because they're not. He's great that way. He also offers guidance as to what he thinks is effective and important. He says we must talk with the Chinese, that dialog is important. He really wants students on their campuses to be talking to Chinese student groups, so that they understand the issues and that our fight is not with them. He's a historian, as well as everything else, and knows the value of student movements in social change, whether it's civil rights, apartheid, or Prague Spring.

There's a whole generation of Tibetans, both in and out of Tibet, who have never known an independent Tibet. They don't know what life was like before the Chinese and can never recapture the Tibet of our parents' or grandparents' memories. Yet, despite the government's attempt to wipe out our culture, people are struggling for a freedom they have never known. It may take a while, but I absolutely believe I'll see a free Tibet in my lifetime.

LINKS

www.tibet.org/SFT

▶ 34.

Notes on Tibet
1949-1959

| TENZIN TSETAN CHOKLAY |

In the year 1949, the People's Liberation Army (PLA) began its long march into Tibet. By October of the following year, some 40,000 Chinese troops attacked the eastern province and defeated the 8,000-man Tibetan army. A month later, due to the emergency, the 14th Dalai Lama, although a 15-year-old minor, was compelled to assume full political authority as head of state.

Threatened with further military invasion, in May 1951 Tibetan delegates in Beijing were forced to sign the infamous 17-Point 'Agreement' on Measures for the Peaceful Liberation of Tibet. It is noted that in the same month, a more favorable treaty was attempted with China, but all proposals were turned down.

The large-scale Tibetan National Uprising broke out in Lhasa (the capital of Tibet) in March 1959. The demonstrations were ruthlessly, and in the most severe manner, crushed by the PLA; about 87,000 Tibetans were killed. The ever-deteriorating circumstances led the Dalai Lama to flee to exile in India. Later in the same month of that year, Chinese Premier Zhou Enlai announced the termination of the Tibetan government.

The Dalai Lama and the thousands of Tibetans who followed him reestablished the Tibetan Government in Exile in India, where it has been functioning since 1959. The Tibetan people recognize this exiled government as the true government of Tibet.

▶ 35.

Rape, Forced Relocation, Labor, and Poverty
Stories That Must Be Told

| KA HSAW WA |

Ka Hsaw Wa

I was a very obnoxious teenager. I was the youngest of the family, the center of love. I didn't care about anybody but myself. All I wanted to do was to spend money, wear nice clothes, and hang out.

My life changed when I was 17 years old. One of my closest friends, who opposed the military government in Burma, ran away. I didn't have any idea where he went. The military wanted information from me that I couldn't provide, so they tortured me for three days, nonstop. It was such a painful thing for me — more psychologically than physically. I was so angry!

The Burmese government had screwed up many things in our country, so I started organizing students to participate in the movement for democracy and freedom. I wasn't thinking we would change our country; I knew the only thing we could change were the minds of the youth. When the student uprisings began, my friends and I would go around the school and give speeches to the students, urging them to participate in our movement. Slowly, a lot of students from other schools joined with our demonstrations, and we spread throughout Burma.

But instead of getting what we asked for — a government that would negotiate with us — they just shot down our students and demonstrators. Many of my friends were killed right in front of me. Then they started arresting people, putting them in jail, and torturing them.

I knew they would come after me, because they knew I was one of the organizers. I didn't want to leave, but I didn't know where to go and I didn't have any money. So, I hid in a nearby village and tried to keep in touch with my mom. Finally, after two weeks she came to see me. She told me there was no way I could go home, because they were after me and had already arrested some of my friends. So I made the decision that I would leave. My mom gave me some money, I packed my stuff, and went into the jungle toward the Thai border.

At that time, I was so confused and scared and angry. I wanted to go back and kill them, the same way they had killed my friends and the demonstrators. In my mind, I thought I would do it. But while I was walking in the jungle for three days and nights, right before I reached one of the villages, I saw a scene that changed my whole life.

I saw a dead body. A woman's body, with a tree branch in her vagina and her nipples cut off. I saw the body and the tree branch and I thought: Oh my God, how could people treat each other like that? There were four of us, and we looked at her and couldn't speak a word. Finally we covered her. Very soon, we reached a village and asked what had happened to that lady. She was about 24 years old, a nurse, and the villagers said that she had been taken forcibly by the soldiers to go and cure other sick soldiers. Clearly, instead, she had been raped and killed. I was so angry. My mind was telling me to take revenge, yet I didn't want to create more suffering.

The thing that totally convinced me to take the nonviolent path was when I talked to a mother who was brokenhearted because a soldier had forced her to have sex with her own son. Right after that, her son committed suicide. It was then that I realized that more violence would not improve these peoples' lives. If I took revenge, it would only comfort my anger. I also realized that my people, the people of Burma, did not need any more violence. So, I thought: Okay, I'm going to choose nonviolence and document those atrocities by the military and let the world know what they have done. When I started, I had nothing but a pen and a Burmese/English dictionary. Whenever I talked to people, I wrote down the name of the people who persecuted them, the location, the date, and all the important information. But I had to memorize the story, because I had no paper to write it all down. I had nothing.

To survive, I'd help a villager with his farm so I could continue my work. I got rice and food to eat, but the rest I just had to find around. Living in the jungle with a lack of food, so much malaria, no medicine, no warm clothes was horrible. But it wasn't only me — a lot of people had to live that way, so I didn't care. I had courage. I looked at people and thought: Your story's not being told. Your story needs to be told.

Since then, I have documented hundreds of stories. I learned that human rights abuses are directly linked to the exploitation of natural resources and that military dictatorships get money from corporate investments. For example, the area around the Burmese pipeline — owned by Unocal America, Total /France, and the Burmese military dictatorship — is where so many of the human rights violations have happened: rape, forced relocation, forced labor, forced poverty. I talked with so many, many different victims. Soldiers, who themselves had committed violations, who defected from the army, told us lots of stories.

As I interviewed people, I asked whether or not I could use their real names or if they were afraid. I wanted to introduce them to the idea that we could bring about a lawsuit in the United States. Many people wanted to help, until we explained to them about the court system in the United States and the process they would have to go through. After that, a lot of them backed off, because they knew that the military system might be abusive. But 14 of them are in the lawsuit that Earth Rights International has against Unocal now, and it is doing really well in the court system in the US.

One of the stories from our lawsuit is heartbreaking. A woman who lived in a village in the pipeline area was being forced to move. Of course, the lives of these people are so attached to the land, because culturally, after a baby is born they bury the placenta underneath a tree and believe that the God of the Master of Trees will protect their son or daughter. So they didn't want to leave, and they refused. Five soldiers came up to her and started beating and questioning her. She was in front of her home, nursing her two-month-old baby and cooking over a fire when a soldier came and kicked her. The baby fell into the fire and later died. She brought the lawsuit on behalf of her daughter and herself. She is such a strong woman to stand up for her rights.

When I chose nonviolence, lots of people said: You are young and stupid. You just don't have the guts to fight or to die for your people. They said: Why don't you take arms against them and fight; they're killing your people every day? No one supported me.

But I have no courage if I don't tell the truth. I document abuses because I think if I don't keep doing it, what are those people going to do? So many people are doing bad things, and they must be seen.

Now, because of our lawsuit, the United States has a sanction against Burma, and some US cities have purchasing agreements, which means they do not do business with any businesses that invest in Burma. It feels so good to punish the government. For example, I have testified at the International Labor Organization (ILO) many times. Finally they kicked Burma out of their membership. That's so incredible, such a success! And even though the pipeline was finished in 1998, there's not a drop of gas flowing yet. That's because when we learned that the World Bank was going to finance the power plant that was going to receive all the gas from Burma, we fought against it and won.

Now I run a school in Thailand, where we teach indigenous people to protect their rights and environment. We teach them about international and human rights law and about democracy. They learn about networking, fact-finding, writing, and campaigning. They are in school for three months, and then they go back into the field to practice what they've learned. Afterward, they come back to the school; we give them feedback, teach them for another three months, and then they go back in the field again and return. The school project is going very well, and we have finished two terms. Our students have already started their own organizations and are doing a very effective job in Burma, which makes me so happy.

I believe that young people are the power. They often act from pure love and action, not for money or financial gain. And so many want change. As individuals they can do a lot. But to effect change, young people in the US need to know what kind of system they're living in. They need to educate themselves and their friends.

They might think that they have a democratic system, are fully free, but I don't think so.

When I was a youth in Burma, I used to think America was the most beautiful, democratic system in the world. Then I came here, and I learned that the government is totally controlled by the corporations. To me, democracy means the power of the people, the choice of the people. But no, it's the corporations who are in power. It makes me really upset. When people know the issues, though, and know about the country they live in, then they can make changes.

Ka Hsaw Wa (pronounced Kasawa) was born in Rangoon, Burma and currently lives in New York City. Due to his involvement in the pro-democracy student rebellion, he has not seen his family or been home since 1988. He is cofounder of Earth Rights International, which runs a school for activists in Thailand.

LINKS

www.earthrights.org

▶ 36.

Top 200
The Rise of Corporate Global Power

| SARA ANDERSON AND JOHN CAVANAGH |

In a study entitled "Top 200: The Rise of Corporate Global Power," the Institute for Policy Studies examined the economic and political power of the world's largest corporations. (These are the firms that are driving the process of corporate globalization and arguably benefiting the most from it.) The study concluded that widespread trade and investment liberalization have contributed to a climate in which dominant corporations are enjoying increasing levels of economic and political clout that are out of balance with the tangible benefits they provide to society.

The study reinforces a strong public distrust of the economic and political power of corporations. In September 2000, *Business Week* magazine released a *Business Week*/Harris Poll that showed 72 to 82 percent of Americans agreed that, "Business has gained too much power over too many aspects of American life." Seventy-four to 82 percent further agreed that big companies have too much influence over "government policy, politicians, and policymakers in Washington."

KEY FINDINGS

1. Of the 100 largest economies in the world, 51 are corporations; only 49 are countries (based on a comparison of corporate sales and country GDPs).

2. The Top 200 corporations' sales are growing at a faster rate than overall global economic activity. Between 1983 and 1999, their combined sales grew from the equivalent of 25.0 percent to 27.5 percent of World GDP.

3. The Top 200 corporations' combined sales are greater than the combined economies of all countries, minus the biggest ten.

4. The Top 200s' combined sales are 18 times the size of the combined annual income of the 1.2 billion people (24 percent of the total world population) living in severe poverty.

5. While the sales of the Top 200 are the equivalent of 27.5 percent of world economic activity, they employ only 0.78 percent of the world's workforce.

6. Between 1983 and 1999, the profits of the Top 200 firms grew 362.4 percent, while the number of people they employ grew by only 14.4 percent.

7. A full 5 percent of the Top 200s' combined workforce is employed by Wal-Mart, a company notorious for its union-busting and widespread use of part-time workers to avoid paying benefits. The discount retail giant is the top private employer in the world, with

ANOTHER VOICE

People have to have a sense of their own power. If they live in democracies, they've got to begin moving in, taking over political parties — reshaping them. It means they've got to grow up civic. Right now, they're growing up corporate.

— Ralph Nader

1,140,000 workers — more than twice as many as second-place DaimlerChrysler, which employs 466,938 workers.

8. US corporations dominate the Top 200, with 82 slots (41 percent of the total). Japanese firms are second, with only 41 slots.

9. Of the US corporations on the list, 44 did not pay the full, standard 35 percent federal corporate tax rate during the period 1996-1998. Seven of the firms actually paid less than zero in federal income taxes in 1998 (because of rebates). These include: Texaco, Chevron, PepsiCo, Enron, Worldcom, McKesson, and the world's biggest corporation — General Motors.

10. Between 1983 and 1999, the share of total sales of the Top 200 made up by service sector corporations increased from 33.8 percent to 46.7 percent. Gains were particularly evident in financial services and telecommunications sectors, in which most countries have pursued deregulation.

LINKS

www.ips-dc.org

► 37.

The Violence of Globalization

India Pushes Back

| VANDANA SHIVA |

The biggest issue we face in India is the destruction of sustainable small-scale economies, such as agriculture and food production. Most small farms in India are one-half acre to one acre. Farmers grow 100 to 200 crops — large amounts for subsistence use and sale — not just for food but for fiber, color dyeing, fertilizer, pest control, and medicine. Out of that the economy runs.

The entire threat of globalization is basically wiping out these diverse, localized systems — wiping out their biodiversity. It's all being turned around on its head. It's like we're turning the world into a child, born prematurely, who must be kept on life support systems. The global economy is becoming a life support system for the smallest microorganism, for the street or stream, for the village. And it's creating a threat both to the Earth and to livelihoods, creating insecurity on a scale we can't imagine.

It's not true that just because more ships go around the world and more jets fly around the world that we're somehow getting more in life. We are not producing richer, more satisfying lives. We're certainly not producing more food — at least not good food. We might be producing more junk food, but we are not producing more

Vandana Shiva

nutrition. We are not producing more biodiversity. We are not producing more water — the basic things that make us live.

We've got to get out of the mythology of growth that keeps everyone intoxicated. We need to start recognizing the knowledge and productivity of the past. We need to start listening to the voices of the small producer, the small vendor, the small retailer, the small farmer, and the small fisherman — which is a majority of the world. It's also a majority of the women. Out of that comes the truthful resurrection of diversity that gives us the possibility of small-scale, low-impact economies for the Earth and extremely high-impact economies for human security and the future. A majority of the voices — the largest sector — is being ignored just because, individually, they are small. But without them, this world cannot be supported.

Don't listen to the voices of global corporations. Monsanto, for example, came to India about four years ago and started to buy up local seed companies. The result of all that concentration and deregulation has been that farmers are buying more costly seed, are buying more pesticide, and have become more dependent on external inputs. Women in India have always been the seed keepers, but companies like Monsanto, the seed experts, basically take the power of sustaining seed away from them. Women also end up carrying the burden of society, because their husbands usually borrow for the new products, such as chemicals and pesticides. They are getting into such deep debt that hundreds and thousands of small farmers are now starting to commit suicide. The women are left with the farm, the home, the children, and the future. Sometimes husbands sell their kidneys (we have found a huge number of these cases), and then they can't work. And the women are having to look after everything!

We also have Monsanto subverting the environmental laws of the country. All those laws that have ensured the diversity and purity of our food are being destroyed. Two thousand laws relating to food safety, to chemical ingredients, and to insuring that most food is processed at the small, local level have been changed. We've had to take Monsanto to the courts to defend our environmental protection laws and the autonomy of our government.

Companies, such as Monsanto and global institutions such as the WTO aren't just spreading genetic pollution, they're spreading political pollution and knowledge pollution, too. That is the root of growing violence in our society. Our government cannot protect us, because it is forced under the WTO to obey the rules of the international trading system, which prevents it from having any power to act in our behalf. If it does, it is acting against the trade laws, and the country can be sued, fined, and sanctioned against.

In certain situations where this new corporate agriculture and globalization is destroying farming and agriculture, employment is collapsing, and we are finding that there is an absolute explosion of prostitution. Women are selling their bodies to survive. The growth in prostitution is not a choice that women are making. It's the ultimate destitution into which they are being pushed by the forces of globalization. Women would much rather work with nature, produce food, look after communities, and be independent. There are two kinds of survival: First, there's survival with dignity, simplicity, and autonomy. And then there's the kind of survival that globalization is pushing people into — survival with violence, indignity, and total destitution.

Cargill has a major agenda to take over India's entire food distribution system. Now just imagine how large the food distribution system of India must be to feed a billion people. Cargill would like to control the trade in food and to make larger profits by buying cheaply from farmers. But Cargill doesn't produce food — farmers produce food. Yet the entire price support system by which farmers get adequate return to ensure a living wage and a living return is being dismantled, in order to allow Cargill to take over the food trade system. We're fighting very hard against this.

We have two strong women's campaigns, both against Cargill. One is a national alliance on women's food rights, against genetically engineered soil, which the women can't stand. That campaign has involved some dumping actions. The other is against having Cargill enter the staple food system to try and sell extremely over-processed, stale flour under the brand name "Nature Fresh." That movement argues: No! Nature fresh is what nature gives us, not what Cargill gives in rotten flax with pretty plastic packaging.

As for the young people, they are obviously split along a total class line. The young élite, which can service the global corporations, are only thinking of how they can make hundreds and thousands of rupees and get the new special visas to go all over the world. And of course, Indian experts are in demand everywhere. They're being wooed; they're being paid high salaries compared to India's low local salaries.

But there is also a large group of young people that is angry. They feel they are being denied a future. For example, in a remote area of India, 300,000 village and small town youth joined hands to lock out a Pepsi plant, to say we don't want this for our future. No national paper carried it — only Hindi papers. BBC and CNN didn't carry it, either. But 300,000 people! That's much larger than the protests in Seattle. It was a very large mobilization against the destruction of our food culture and the corporate takeover of our economy. And it's no surprise that 300,000 youth in the streets are not news. That's the point of globalization — that millions do not matter. Millions can be rendered invisible and voiceless. That is the violence of globalization.

I always say globalization can only thrive on the grave of democracy. So we ask the people in the North to discipline their governments and their corporations. Seattle was a start. We are strong enough to fight violence in our own societies ourselves. What we need you to do is stop your companies at home. Have a movement to stop Cargill from taking over our food system. You don't have to come to India and tell us how our farmers should behave. You need to tell Cargill how it should behave. You need to tell your state department how it should behave. You need to tell your commerce department. The day you resurrect democracy in the US, we resurrect democracy here.

Dr. Vandana Shiva is a physicist, ecologist, activist, editor, and author of many books. In India she has established "Navdanya," a movement for biodiversity conservation and farmers' rights. She directs the Research Foundation for Science, Technology, and Ecology and is on the board for the International Forum on Globalization.

LINKS

www.ifg.org

▶ 38.

Factory Farms, Slaughterhouses, and Laboratories

Compassion over Killing

| PAUL SHAPIRO |

▲

Paul Shapiro

I was 13 years old when I first watched undercover footage taken by investigators at factory farms, slaughterhouses, and laboratories. As soon as I saw that footage I knew something was dramatically and fundamentally wrong with what I had been taught about human/ non-human relations. One species (human beings) has assumed moral superiority over another, the way that whites have assumed color superiority or men have presumed gender superiority. We wear animals, eat animals, ride animals. We use them for labor; we use them for entertainment. We experiment on them. And we don't have any ethical qualms about doing it, regardless of whether or not it's necessary.

STEVE CUCOLO

Animals are so defenseless, so powerless and so voiceless that it is our duty — our moral obligation — to provide them with a voice. If you ask anybody on the street if they are opposed to causing unnecessary suffering to animals, you'll get a resounding Yes! But many of those same people will wear fur or leather. They'll eat meat or animal products. They'll use cosmetics that have been tested on animals.

In order to get people to think and act differently toward other species, as animal activists, we need to say: Look, here is a video of an undercover investigation that we did at this slaughterhouse. Here's the way that your meat is produced. You see it in a cellophane package; it looks nice and neat. You don't see the face of the animal; you don't hear its cries; you don't smell the stench of the slaughterhouse. Look into factory farming; you'll see that many of these places are fortresses of security. They have video cameras, barbed wire fences, and locked doors. They hide from the public. If we expose them and appeal to people's consciences, I think a revolution would be forged.

We show people the reality of the egg industry, for instance. Hens are kept in battery cages — small, wire mesh cages crammed with four to six hens each — and treated as commodities. They spend one to three years of their lives in these tiny cages. They can't spread their wings. They can't breathe fresh air. They never see natural light or touch dirt. Oftentimes their toes grow around the cage wire, keeping them stuck in one place. They become aggressive, which is why the industry shears off a portion of the hens' beaks — with no anesthetic!

ANOTHER **VOICE**

Marching around with a sign is one thing, but you must also try to live your life according to what the sign you hold says.
— Brett Munckton

Why Not?
You eat other animals,
don't you?
GO VEGETARIAN

Videos can be very powerful. That's why at Compassion over Killing, we started taking a portable TV/VCR to our protests. When we show a video of animals being anally electrocuted for their fur, branded on their faces, and torched alive in medical research, then people start to pay attention to the message. When I see how upset people get watching images of institutionalized animal cruelty, it makes me feel better about our species as a whole.

Most people who become interested in animal rights start with vegetarianism. Then they learn about what the egg and dairy industries are doing, and they start removing their support. They learn about what medical labs are doing and start boycotting cosmetics that are tested on animals. It's a gradual process. Like many other people, I didn't make dramatic changes overnight. Nobody can be reasonably expected to change their entire lifestyle like that.

Unlike other social justice struggles, to believe in animal rights means you really have to change a lot about the way you live. If somebody wants to join the anti-death penalty movement, they just have to change the way they think. But they don't have to change what they eat, what they wear, the type of entertainment they support, or the

cosmetics that they buy. Animal rights activism is an all-pervasive lifestyle change.

I think it is important to treat people who abuse animals with the same amount of compassion and respect we think they ought to extend to animals. Passing harsh judgments on people won't do anything to get them to change. What we need to do is set an example by leading compassionate lifestyles that will make other people want to do the same. This is hard, sometimes. Because when you see the misery animals are forced to endure, you just want to scream: Hey, stop! Stop supporting this killing; stop supporting this violence. But oftentimes that's a very unproductive and ineffective thing to do.

When I say we ought to treat animal abusers with compassion, I guess I should make it clear that the views I'm expressing are my own and not those of the movement. That belief is not shared by all of my colleagues. There's disagreement in this movement, as in any other. But in my view, nobody is incapable of change, and I don't want to treat people as if they were enemies of the movement. I try to think everybody I meet is 'pre-vegan.' As an activist, I need to constantly assess whether or not I am doing enough. More often than not, the answer is: No, I need to be doing more.

Paul Shapiro is the founder and codirector of Compassion over Killing, Washington, DC's only grassroots animal rights organization. A nonprofit organization founded in 1995, Compassion over Killing believes in granting basic rights to sentient non-human animals and, therefore, in ending institutionalized animal exploitation.

LINKS

www.cok-online.org

▶ 39.

Force-Fed
The Tyranny of Corporate Agribusiness

| JOHN E. PECK |

JOHN NICHOLS; COURTESY OF CAPITAL TIMES

▲

*John E. Peck (left)
and José Bové (right)*

I first realized that corporate agribusiness is out to destroy the family farm when I learned to ride a bike. Growing up on a 260-acre (105-hectare) farm in central Minnesota meant a three-mile (five-kilometer) trek just to go 'around the block.' I soon encountered all sorts of unfamiliar names on the signposts: Sandoz, Ciba-Geigy, Pfizer, Land O'Lakes, and Cargill. Since none of them were neighbors I knew, I asked my parents who owned so much land.

The truth of the matter was that our big neighbors were legal fictions, making money off peddling hybrid seeds, synthetic fertilizers, pesticides, hormones, etc. As faceless corporations, they had little care for soil quality, biodiversity, food safety, animal welfare, or even the well-being of the farm families and the rural towns they preyed upon. When some of our neighbors went bankrupt and took their own lives, I blamed the agribusiness outfits that created dependency, rigged prices, manipulated markets, and extracted profit without regard for people's lives.

Later, when I joined Future Farmers of America (FFA), I was force-fed all sorts of corporate propaganda: Get big or get out. Food is a weapon. Plant fence row to fence row. Become an agribusinessman. That pressure to conform got even worse when I went to the University of Wisconsin-Madison (a land grant college). There, agribusiness dictated classroom curriculum and drove taxpayer-subsidized research.

Our activist group, the UW Greens, finally started a campaign to educate others about how biotech research was hurting both farmers and consumers. We posted warnings on vending machines and leafleted campus cafeterias. Within days, Monsanto was in the media attacking us as ecoterrorists, and one dean even publicly called us neo-Luddites! Whenever an authority figure resorts to such name-calling, you know you are on the right track.

Although farmers have traditionally bred plants and animals for eons, today's genetic engineering is quite different, since it no longer respects barriers between species. We now have bacteria spliced into potatoes, fish genes stuck into tomatoes, even bear genes inserted into salmon! And according to the USDA, over 98 percent of this genetic tinkering is done to make agricultural production and processing more profitable — not to make food healthier or more nutritious.

Cows injected with bovine growth hormone (rBGH), for example, produce much more milk than usual. But that milk has higher levels of insulin-like growth factor (IGF-1), known to cause colon, breast and prostate cancer; as well as elevated antibiotic residues (since injected cows are more susceptible to udder infections). rBGH 'burns out' cows quickly, and contaminated carcasses end up in hamburgers, tacos, and as high-protein feed for other livestock (potentially leading to epidemics such as mad cow disease). Surveys have shown that the vast majority of farmers and consumers do not want rBGH, yet this biotechnology is still being pushed by corporations such as Kraft, who are interested in having as much cheap milk as possible.

Natural ecosystems suffer from runaway biotech research, too. Gene-jumping has already created superweeds that are resistant to pesticides, and drifting Bt corn pollen has contaminated organic fields downwind, wiping out non-target species like monarch butterflies and lacewings. Genetically modified soil fungi sprayed on coca and marijuana as part of the war on drugs now threatens to attack food crops and other plants throughout Latin America. Agriculture is too important to leave in the greedy hands of corporations. Corporate cheerleaders want you to think your next meal will be another carefree biotech wonder product – but don't believe the hype.

Two-thirds of US family farmers have disappeared since World War II and three to four farmers still go under in Wisconsin every week. Yet this trend is neither inevitable nor irreversible. Across the globe, family farmers still persist, using diverse low-input systems that are often more productive and certainly more sustainable than the dubious cornucopia promised by corporate agribusiness. For example, in southern France, the struggle against *la mal bouffe* (junk food) is growing more and more serious as people reject homogenized corporate junk food in favor of organic, locally grown alternatives and as family farmers rebel against the global free trade regimes like the WTO. José Bové (a family farmer) became a national hero there when he damaged part of a McDonald's with his tractor and was subsequently jailed. Bové raises sheep and makes Roquefort cheese, near the town of Millau. When France refused to import US beef that was laced with hormones, the US (sanctioned by the WTO) retaliated by imposing heavy tariffs on selected agricultural products — among them, gourmet French cheeses such as Roquefort.

Bové has since traveled to Brazil and led peasant farmers there in destroying a thousand acres of genetically modified corn and soybeans at a Monsanto field trial station. He maintains that he is only acting in self-defense against irresponsible corporations that are forcing family farmers to grow (and consumers to eat) food they don't want.

Where I grew up, people still recognize a happy earthworm when they see it, and they appreciate the differences among rhubarb varieties. Wholesome healthy food is a basic human right, and family farmers around the globe deserve our support in their struggle to defend it.

John E. Peck is a graduate student in the Land Resources Program of the Institute of Environmental Studies at the University of Wisconsin-Madison. His current PhD research is on sustainable agriculture and community-based natural resource management in Zimbabwe.

▶ 40.

Eliminating Slavery in Agricultural Labor
The Coalition of Immokalee Workers

| ROMEO RAMIREZ - TRANSLATED BY ALAN SEID |

I started working the day I arrived here from Guatemala, when I was 15 years old. I've picked oranges in Florida and tomatoes in Georgia, Florida and Virginia, often earning less than minimum wage. Today, I work in a watermelon cooperative, which is very different from just being a worker. Now, I also fight for the rights of laborers.

The watermelon cooperative is part of the Coalition of Immokalee Workers, which exists for our benefit to get us more respect from employers, fair and better working conditions, more freedom, and fair pay. As agricultural workers, we are often seen only as machines and not as human beings. Most farm workers earn only 40 cents for every 32-pound (15-kilogram) bucket they pick, which is essentially the same as it was 20 years ago. Many of the working conditions we live with are illegal and have been eliminated in other industries: forced

Romeo Ramirez
(third from the left)

COURTESY OF COALITION OF IMMOKALEE WORKERS

labor, extortion, dangerous working conditions, stagnated wages, and no right to form unions. Because of these conditions and the hard and heavy labor, farm work continues to be a life of misery for many.

I found out about the Coalition when I went through a situation where I didn't get paid. I found out that the state's legal services couldn't help me, so I asked around for someone who could help me file a complaint and get paid. I was told about the Coalition and that they had meetings every Wednesday, so I went and I saw that it was all workers who were talking about how it wasn't fair to be paid the same amount as 20 years ago.

At the meetings, they said they wanted to change the balance of power between the workers and bosses. They were talking about how they had done an analysis of the industry and working conditions and that they planned strikes to end the mistreatment happening. I saw that the Coalition was different from other organizations, because there was not just one leader; everyone was a leader. That's when I decided to get more involved. I started volunteering and participating in the actions, in committees, and in planning meetings, to see how we could resolve the miserable conditions for workers like me.

In order to achieve some of the changes we wanted, we had general strikes to show that we are not work machines and to tell the bosses we're not satisfied with the salaries they are paying. We had a march against violence, where 600 people walked to the house of a contractor who had beaten a worker for going to get water while on the job. We wanted the contractor to know that to beat one worker is to beat all workers. We did a month-long hunger strike to bring to the public's attention what the life of a worker is like, and we had a 230-

mile-long (370-kilometer-long) march for respect for workers. We marched so we could have face-to-face dialogs with the companies where worker's voices are rejected. We have given press conferences, where we explained our campaigns and presented copies of the letters we had sent to the large corporations asking them to intervene to change things.

We talked with our representatives and senators about the poor conditions for workers, so that they would realize poverty isn't just in other countries but right here in North America. We wanted

the senators to resolve the wrongs and fix the laws they create that exploit us. We also marched to the Florida governor's mansion to request more fairness and to ask him to intervene between the workers and bosses. Most importantly, we wanted to bring public awareness to the lack of economic justice.

I volunteered for two years with the watermelon cooperative and when the general assembly met, they voted to make me a member of the staff. To this date, I've been in the central part of the organization and actions.

As part of our organization's program to eliminate slavery in agricultural labor in Florida, I've secretly investigated violent slavery operations. I worked side by side with workers, picking fruit with them, investigating and asking them questions about the situation with their bosses, who forced them to stay and work when they wanted to go work somewhere else. Because of actions like this, we have succeeded in getting convictions against farm labor recruiters and labor contractors who exploit migrant workers by kidnapping, extorting, robbing, abusing, and enslaving them.

Agricultural workers get paid less than $7,500 per year and have no legal right to earn overtime or bargain collectively with employers. Recently, we started a campaign against Taco Bell. Taco Bell is a multinational corporation that makes billions and billions of dollars on the backs of farm workers and indigenous people, because they can get away with buying cheap ingredients and paying below-poverty wages. When you look at the difference in power between us as farm workers and Taco Bell as a billion-dollar corporation, you may think we are crazy for taking them on. They have all the wealth and political power, and we have only one weapon. But that weapon — the truth — is the most powerful thing on Earth, so we are certain that we will prevail.

Many students, religious and labor leaders, and people from our community are joining us to call for a boycott to end 'sweatshops in the fields.' And because of the Coalition, we have developed a powerful political voice at the state level. There is no doubt that we have brought a lot of attention to the wrongful situation of agricultural workers in Florida, and we are going to keep working until we have achieved fairness, respect, and an end to the human injustice.

At the age of 9, Romeo Ramirez starting planting sugarcane and doing field work to support his family. He came to the United States when he was 15, because of the economic and political conditions existing in his country.

LINKS

www.ciw-online.org

▶ 41.

Wake Up and Smell the Exploitation

The Campaign for Fair Trade, Certified Coffee

| MAY CASTRO |

DANIEL QUIGLEY AND NICOLE DEMIGLIO

▲

May Castro

I began concentrating on global issues because of the plethora of students who don't know how others live beyond their middle class towns of Northern Virginia. With the help and support of Oxfam, TransFair USA, and CHANGE, I have been able to start a campaign for Fair Trade Certified Coffee on my college campus.

Coffee is the second most heavily traded commodity in the world. Just one cup of it manifests global issues such as hunger, poverty, social injustice, and environmental degradation. Many people in the United States spend more than $3.00 a day on their caffeine cravings, but few know that the average coffee farmer earns less than $1.00 a day. The $18 billion a year Americans spend on coffee requires the labor of 20 million people, including women and children, who work as many as 14 hours a day under harsh conditions on coffee plantations for pay that wouldn't even buy them a cup of coffee here.

And coffee does not just affect people; it affects the Earth. More than 70 percent of the world's coffee is sprayed with synthetic chemicals, such as Malathion and DDT, which not only pollutes the water and soil and poisons the food chain, but also results in infertile and depleted land. With such a high demand for their product, plantation owners have destroyed millions of acres of forests to provide direct sunlight for the coffee plants to grow faster.

Fair Trade Certified Coffee seeks to improve the lives of coffee farmers by guaranteeing a fair price for their harvests, providing access to affordable credit, and promoting sustainable practices, such as organic farming. These coffee farmers are guaranteed a minimum of $1.26 per pound ($2.77 per kilogram) for their coffee, compared to the average $0.07 per pound ($0.15 per kilogram). They also receive an additional $0.15 per pound ($0.33 per kilogram) premium if the coffee is certified organic.

Fair Trade Certified Coffee also helps protect the environment. By supporting farmers to grow their crops in the shade, wildlife habitat is preserved. And the coffee retains a higher quality taste. In the United States, most Fair Trade Coffee in 1999 was certified organic, making it the most environmentally friendly coffee available.

Fair Trade organizations bypass exploitative middlemen and work directly with producers, representing 21 countries throughout Latin America, Asia, and Africa. Three hundred Fair Trade cooperatives, representing 550,000 farmers and their families, sell through the Fair Trade Register.

The Fair Trade Coffee campaign that I started on my campus not only gives coffee farmers the benefits of tactful advocacy; it also gives me the opportunity to educate others on how their consumer decisions can help change the world. Convincing people to switch to Fair Trade Coffee helps delink the connection between cheap labor and coffee growing and forces the industry to think more responsibly about their workers and the environment.

May Castro is a student at George Mason University, where she is involved with peace and justice work. A poster she drew of the Fair Trade Certified label with the words "Buy Fair Trade Coffee" hangs outside her apartment window.

LINKS

www.transfairusa.org

▶ 42.

Union Organizing in El Salvador

In Solidarity with US Students

| SONIA BEATRIZ LARA - TRANSLATED BY BARBARA BRIGGS|

There are a lot of risks to organizing workers in the San Marcos Free Trade Zone. Principally, you can lose your job, which is what happened to me in 1999 after I spoke with a visiting delegation of students from Columbia University. At the time, I did not think of the risks; my courage came from the many injustices that I experienced and witnessed while working in the factory.

The supervisors and Korean bosses at Doall Enterprises were exploiting us greatly. The more we produced, the more they wanted us to increase production. In spite of the fact that we were keeping up with their increased demands, they would mistreat us, both physically and verbally — pressuring us. Always telling us: Hurry up; hurry up and produce more.

Most people felt that they couldn't react: if there was any union effort whatsoever, the workers would get fired — 15 or 20 at a time. I have only one child, but most of the women have many children and just couldn't take the risk of losing their jobs.

In November 1999, a group met and tried to form the first union in Doall. They were fired immediately; only one founding member was left inside the factory. That's when the National Labor

Sonia Beatriz Lara

BARBARA BRIGGS

Committee pressured the American company who, in turn, pressured Doall to reinstate the workers.

So, there was pressure and a negotiation. After three months, 30 of the workers were reinstated — with back wages. Doall signed an agreement: there would be no reprisals and reinstated workers would not be fired again. Further, no discrimination inside the factory was to be allowed, so that others could speak with union workers inside the factory and not be fired themselves. From the time of the reinstatement, the Ministry of Labor required a six-month period before the union could be established. In August, a new union was constituted, called SETDESA.

Now that the union leadership is in place, it works to protect union members from being fired and negotiates with the management to improve other aspects of the factory. For example, before, you had to go into work at ten minutes to seven. If you didn't, the supervisors would deduct a half-hour from your wages or they'd send you home. Now the workers just go in at seven o'clock. Previously, workers had no break from seven in the morning until noon. Now there's a 15-minute break at nine-thirty.

SETDESA is the only functioning union in the *maquilla* (factory) right now in the Free Trade Zone Assembly for Export sector. Union organizers talk with legal representatives of the factory and look for ways to come to an agreement, even though a collective contract doesn't exist. (In El Salvador you're allowed to form a union with 30 memberships, which gives certain legal recognition and protection. But to officially negotiate a collective contract, union leaders need to have a membership of 51 percent, which we don't have yet.)

I believe that the union's existence and its continued growth is exclusively due to the effective US pressure and involvement of US people — in particular, the students. It is very moving to know that even though they don't live in our country, young people joined us in our fight against the suffering we endured in the *maquillas*. Their solidarity has had a great impact and been very important to our movement.

▼

Sonia Beatriz Lara has given testimony in the United States on sweatshop conditions and is currently employed by the National Labor Committee as an inspector, investigating conditions in the factories and helping to grow the union at Doall Enterprises in El Salvador.

▶ 43.

Exposed
The Truth Behind the Label

| CHARLES KERNAGHAN |

▲

Charles Kernaghan

T he issue of sweatshop labor has exploded on college and high school campuses across the country because the workers making the products that young people buy are young people themselves — so there's an immediate bond. The workforce in many areas of the world is made up of people aged 16 to 25, over 80 percent of whom are women. So when I go to campuses I take photographs with me, so that students can see for themselves that these workers are not only their same age, they're often much younger.

I tell students to go home and look in their closets. When they do, they'll see that 70 percent of all the apparel we purchase in the United States are imports from Bangladesh, China, and Mexico. Eighty percent of sporting goods and 90 percent of shoes and sneakers are imports. We're in the global economy, I say, but do you ever stop to imagine who makes these products and under what circumstances? How old is the person who made this shirt? What is she paid? Are her rights respected? How does she live? What does she eat? Why are the workers in this factory so young? Why don't the companies hire her parents or her older brothers or sisters? Do the workers have the right to organize? It's through that very questioning process that society can transform.

| 189 |

So the role of young people, very simply, is to ask the serious questions and become the voice of the voiceless. If corporations are going to be held accountable, to respect human rights, women's rights, and to pay fair wages, then young people are going to have to get involved and use their power. For example, when a large company is criticized by a union, they can turn to the mainstream media and say: You can't believe a thing the unions say. They're paid to attack us; that's their job. The media, by and large, believes that. And the media in the United States is completely anti-union. It's so prejudiced and biased, it's incredible. But when students go to the corporations and ask the same questions, the companies can't point to the students and say: They're a special interest group paid to attack us; they're only after money.

Annually, the National Labor Committee (NLC) sponsors a permitted holiday candlelight march and vigil in New York. We start in front of Niketown and march down Fifth Avenue to the infamous Christmas tree at Rockefeller Center. Last year, 3,500 people came; 2,000 of them were high school students. No one's ever seen anything like it. When that many students march down Fifth Avenue, nothing (not even boycotts) terrifies the companies more.

In fact, NLC doesn't advocate boycotts. Almost any worker in the world will tell you it's better to be exploited and have a job than to have no job at all. Of course, we supported the boycott in South Africa against apartheid and in Burma against the military dictatorship, but we don't support them in factories in China, Honduras, or Nicaragua.

I find that in general, sweatshop workers around the world don't know their rights. They are caught in a trap, locked behind barbed wire in factories with armed guards and locked metal gates

with 15-foot-high cinderblock walls. They've never heard of the US companies they ultimately work for; they don't know what kind of profits are being made; and they don't know what wages are being paid elsewhere in the world.

In El Salvador, there are 229 factories, employing 79,000 workers who send us over 600 million garments a year. Eighty-three percent are women, and 50 percent of those are single mothers. Despite pregnancy tests, 60-cent-per-hour wages that only meet one-third of the cost of living, despite forced overtime, heat, filthy water, and all sorts of abuse, there's only one union in the entire country in any of these factories.

The workers know they are being violated. They may not know all the legal rights of the country, but they know they shouldn't be forced to work overtime at the last minute. They know that they have the right to use the bathroom (they're usually limited to using it twice a day in the factories). They know that they shouldn't be spit at or fondled or hit.

BARBARA BRIGGS

The first principle of all of our campaigns is to keep jobs in the developing world, but to keep them with dignity, respect, and justice. This is very difficult, due to enormous unemployment. In Nicaragua, for instance, women are told there are 200 people lined up waiting to take their jobs. The bosses tell the women: I don't need

I WANT TO
END
CHILD
LABOR
AND
SWEAT
SHOP
ABUSES

COURTESY OF THE NATIONAL LABOR COMMITTEE

you. You're nothing to me. You're a piece of shit. They actually say to them: Go get yourself a miniskirt, because you're going to be a hooker on the street if you leave here.

Another reason I don't advocate boycotts is because I don't believe we have the right to tell people what they can and cannot buy. When you have people in this country earning less than $12 an hour, they have no choice but to shop at Wal-Mart. We need to remember that poverty knows no borders.

So, it's very hard. And one of the hardest parts is when people wake up to the issue and ask: So what can we buy? What are the good companies? Well, there aren't any good companies. The statement, "Power corrupts; absolute power corrupts absolutely" is true for these companies that have run wild for so long in this race to the bottom.

In response, the National Labor Committee has come up with I Care shopper's cards for people to leave with the store management when they buy goods. One purpose of the cards is to have people advocate for public disclosure in order to expose industry practices.

The critical issue of public disclosure was championed by students after they went to the factories and saw the machine guns, sawed-off shotguns, and magnum pistols. They saw the barbed wire, locked gates, and the little peepholes. And it was so clear that these companies had something to hide.

Students responded by forming United Students Against Sweatshops (USAS) in 1998. Today, USAS has over 200 campus groups worldwide and is the strongest human rights movement in the US. I don't see anything quite comparable. It's vibrant and it's growing. It needs to deepen. We need to find a better way of working with the developing world. But we're having an enormous impact. The

International Labor Organization tells us that the world is watching USAS and the NLC to see how far we're going to take these campaigns.

The hard part now is keeping the movement alive until there are specific answers. We've come a long way in exposing sweatshop conditions — that's been the great achievement. The sweatshop issue, child labor, and starvation wages can't be hidden any longer. But, we can only keep denouncing these horrible conditions so long, before we move to viable solutions.

We believe that companies will have to respond to us. We know they fear us, because they realize this is a battle for the hearts and minds of the American people. They know this is a moral campaign to get the companies to just do the right thing. They can treat these workers with respect. They can pay them better wages. Human rights, women's rights, and workers' rights must and will be recognized.

▼

Charles Kernaghan is director of the National Labor Committee (NLC), an independent, nonprofit human rights organization focused on sweatshop labor and the protection of workers' rights — especially those of the young women assembling garments and other products for export to the US in Central America, the Caribbean, China, and other developing countries.

LINKS

www.nlcnet.org
www.usanet.org

▶ 44.

Branded
Breaking Out of the Corporate Corral

| NAOMI KLEIN |

▲

Naomi Klein

BRYCE DUFFY

All my life I have been involved in social justice issues — I come from a very political family. In the mid-'90s, when I started doing research for *No Logo* (Picador, 2000), many people of my generation and the generation older than me felt extraordinarily hopeless about the possibility for social change. Partly, it had to do with the feeling that the traditional ways activists had gained a measure of power in society were no longer working. And part of it had to do with a kind of consensus that corporations were more powerful than governments. Our own governments were constantly telling us that ever since the recession in the late '80s and early '90s, there was really very little they could do. That, really, their job was basically to get out of the way of the market; that they were at the mercy of these corporations who could move so easily across borders. This was a real crisis for activism, since traditionally activists go after governments.

Around this time, I started to notice a new spirit of activism. It came particularly from young people, who had grown up knowing that multinational corporations were more powerful than governments. Rather than being paralyzed and confused by this idea, as people of my generation or my parents' generation seemed to be, they were very practical about it. They realized that if power had shifted from the government to the corporation, then they just had to go after the corporations directly. I call this 'hand to brand' combat.

A flurry of brand-based, anti-sweatshop activism began. Rather than attack the issue of sweatshop labor all over the world as a policy question for governments, activists went after brand-name companies like Nike or a brand-named celebrity like Kathy Lee Gifford and turned them into celebrity examples of this problem. Essentially, they used the power of marketing and branding against itself.

Now we're seeing that tactic used over and over again. If activists want to fight against genetic engineering and modification, they not only go after multinationals like Monsanto, Cargill, and Novartis, they also follow the logo until they get to a consumer product that is heavily marketed — like Kellogg's Cornflakes. Then they use the power of marketing against itself. For instance, Greenpeace has a campaign where they parody Tony the Tiger, from Kellogg's, as 'FrankenTony.'

One of the reasons why young people started going after corporations directly had to do with a new kind of anger about the loss of cultural and mental space through corporate marketing. In a sense, high visibility companies — such as Coke and Pepsi, McDonald's, Nike, Adidas, and the Gap — were feeding off of youth culture in a way that they never had before, essentially devouring youth culture and youth spaces, sponsoring every possible piece of youth culture, whether sports or music. They were getting into public spaces, which previously didn't have any advertising (high school classrooms, for instance), through initiatives like Channel 1 and Youth Marketing Systems (YMS).

In a sense, our politics of the late '80s and early '90s was a politics of representation. We thought that if we could fix all of the stereotypes and have a mass culture that represented the true diversity of who we were, then social equality would follow. We thought we could solve all of our problems through media representation, because we were the children of the media. But there was clearly a shift with this new generation of activists. They were not saying: I want to change the pictures in the ads. Or, I want to change the quality of the representation. Instead, they were saying: I want there to be spaces where there's no advertising at all.

In looking at the way advertising was expanding into all of our public spaces, I came across this idea that gripped the corporate world throughout the '90s. It can be summed up in a single phrase that you hear repeated in management circles, business books, magazines, and so on: Brands, not products.

Traditionally, a company would produce a product that people wanted (or that they wanted people to want), and then they would brand it with a logo — an identity that said something about the product. Something like it was high quality, dependable, cool, or could be associated with a lifestyle of some kind. That's traditional branding.

But then, companies decided to come up with brand ideas that were much more powerful than a simple description of their product. From a company like Nike you would hear: We're not a sneaker company. We are about the idea of empowerment through sports. Their slogan "Just Do It" sums up an attitude toward life. A company like Starbucks sells coffee, but not really. What they really do is sell a lifestyle that has to do with community and an attitude toward art and culture — the café culture. They're selling this kind of self-enclosed lifestyle that says more about the people who go to

Starbucks than it says about the coffee. In other words, the logo totally usurped the product. And it's not only the logo that gets branded, it's us — our entire culture, our bodies. We brand ourselves with the identity of these consumer products.

When a company decides that they are about one of these powerful ideas like community or empowerment or democracy, they need ever more cultural space on which to express that brand idea. So, for a company like Starbucks, that means launching a lifestyle magazine, called *Joe*, where coffee is not the main thing. This process of branding is not about advertising a product; it's about creating three-dimensional branded environments where you crawl inside the brand identity. Like a Niketown, it's so much more than a store.

Sold Out America
banner drop

This process that I've been describing has become the new manufacturing of our age. Companies believe that by building a superstore, by launching a lifestyle magazine and sending out powerful messages into the culture, they are producing their product.

So on the one hand, we lose more and more cultural space to branding. On the other hand, this process is enormously expensive, far more expensive than simply advertising a product. What these companies have done over and over again — and this is what I document in my book — is they have funded this foray into lifestyle branding by getting out of the traditional process manufacturing which was the production of their own goods in their own factories. Instead, they contract out.

A company like Nike, which is sort of the original lifestyle brand now in youth culture, doesn't own a single one of its factories. All of its shoes and clothes are produced through a global web of contractors and subcontractors. And the same is now becoming true of Levi's, who have closed at least 22 factories in the last few years. They don't reopen those factories in Mexico or China; instead, they turn those jobs into contracts that Levi's places with contractors. So, more and more, brand-based companies work very hard to make sure that they don't actually directly employ their workforce.

At the mall, this translates into selling through franchises. It means that their goods are sold by young people between the ages of 18 and 24. And then, to make matters worse, they tell those young people: This isn't a real job. This is just a job for you to make a little bit of extra pocket money. More and more companies are relying on temporary labor to keep their costs down.

We are being told by these companies that we can't expect steady employment from them, that they can't provide a manufacturing base for our cities or real jobs for us. That makes these companies very vulnerable. In fact, by breaking the employment contract, they have freed up a generation of activists to say: Wait a minute. I don't like how your products are being produced. I don't like the fact that my school is being invaded by ads. I don't like the way you're treating me.

I believe that it's through these very uncomfortable juxtapositions between image and reality that a lot of young people have taught themselves to understand the global economy, which is enormously complex and hard to understand. It's why there's been an evolution from going after a single corporation like Nike, to going further and learning about institutions like the World Trade Organization and the International Monetary Fund, which are at the root of the problem.

One of the values of these anti-corporate campaigns has been their value as popular education tools to help us understand how the global economy works. If you go to a 13-year-old kid and say: Today we're going to talk about GATT, the General Agreements on Tariffs and Trades, and how that affects the garment industry — they're not going to be that interested. But if you do what Charlie Kernaghan from the National Labor Committee does — which is to hold up a pair of Disney pajamas and say: This is what it costs at Wal-Mart, and this is what a worker in Haiti got paid to make it, and this is what the CEO of Disney got paid last year — then you actually see the disparities in the global economy.

The evolution of this movement is to get much deeper into the entire paradigm of seeking economic growth at all cost. It's about thinking of ways to regulate transnational capital, across the board — which is what these protests of the World Trade Organization, the Free Trade Area of the Americas, etc. is all about. I don't think you change the world one corporation at a time, and most activists know that. The evolution from brand-based, single corporate campaigns to going after the system much more broadly is a significant and hopeful evolution.

Naomi Klein is a writer, journalist, and activist. Her book, No Logo: Taking Aim at the Brand Bullies *is a hard-hitting, word-of-mouth sensation. She has been writing vigorously on the anti-corporate, anti-globalization movement.*

45.

Protecting the Commons
The Struggle for International Water Rights

| MAUDE BARLOW |

GORDON KING

Maude Barlow

At the Council of Canadians, we've shifted from being concerned with nation-state sovereignty to a concern about the sovereign rights of people around the world. We believe we must recapture and protect the commons — those areas of human rights and environmental integrity that are necessary for survival. We think they should be taken back out of the private sphere, decommodified, deprivatized, removed from trade agreements, and put back in the hands of democratic systems. Water must be considered in that process.

Once a part of the commons, water is becoming a commodity nearly as valued and as scarce as oil. Even though we've been in the habit of believing that there is an infinite supply of water on the planet, that assumption is tragically false. The amount of available fresh water is finite — less than $1/2$ of 1 percent of the world's total stock — about what it's been for a million years. The rest is seawater or is inaccessible in polar ice caps, groundwater, and soil.

The reality is that we have taken water wildly for granted. But all is not well. Nearly five million people, mostly children, die every year of water-borne diseases. In the maquiladora zones of Mexico, water is so scarce that babies and children drink Coca-Cola and Pepsi instead. In some countries, aquifers are being depleted so quickly that more water is being taken in a day than can be replenished in 100 years. We are diverting it, polluting it, and depleting it so fast that according to a conservative estimate, by the year 2025, two-thirds of the world's population will be living without adequate supplies of fresh water, and one-third will be living with no access to clean water whatsoever.

Water belongs to the Earth and to all species and is a basic human right. No one has the right to appropriate it for profit. However, just as people are recognizing that, many governments are backing off from their responsibilities to protect their citizens. Under pressure from multinational corporations, the World Bank, and the WTO, governments are moving to privatize the world's water. This basically means that some will have access to all the clean water they need — including for corporate endeavors like high technology or corporate farming — and others will have no access at all to fresh water. There has been a water war in Bolivia, because the World Bank forced it to privatize it's water, and the company that came in to do it, Bectel, doubled the price. There was an uprising. Martial law was declared, people were killed, and it was reported in the Canadian press as a drug war. But it was not; it was a water war.

It's going to take a strong citizens' movement to come together to protect the world's water resources and define a new water ethic for the 21st century. We've already had an enormous impact on destabilizing institutions like the WTO and the World Bank.

NEVA WELTON

APEC (Asia Pacific Economic Cooperation Forum), for example, is probably on its last legs, it's been so discredited. A lot of that has come from the civil society movement. We have a lot to be proud of — a solid record behind us. But in order to create a sustainable movement, we can't be so busy saving the world that we forget the humanity. If we don't nurture each other, we won't survive.

Maude Barlow, is an activist, author, and National Volunteer Chairperson for the Council of Canadians. She is an outspoken crusader for Canadian sovereignty and citizens' rights and is well known for her fight against the FTAA, NAFTA and the MAI.

LINKS

www.canadians.org

▶ 46.

Capitalism
A Pathology of the Market Economy

| DAVID KORTEN |

▲
David Korten

The term 'capitalism' first came into use in the mid-1800s. Back then, it referred specifically to an economic regime that concentrates control of productive assets in the hands of a few to the exclusion of the many.

Today, capitalists would like us to think that capitalism is synonymous with a market economy and private ownership. By their definition, a market economy must be a 'free market,' with no public rules, which of course means that the most powerful players are able to make their own rules at the expense of the weaker.

Capitalism is actually a pathology of a market economy, which tends to evolve in the absence of adequate governmental regulation and citizen oversight. As capitalism thrives, it kills both the market and democracy, because it's about taking rules off the market. You end up with an unlimited concentration of economic power without accountability and institutions with enough power to reshape the rules of government.

Capitalism also eliminates the rules that maintain the integrity of the financial system, allowing bankers and financial speculators to create money, without limit, for the benefit of the wealthy. Combine this with federal reserve policies, which are explicitly geared to holding wages down and keeping the stock market up, and you can see the clear shift in the balance of wealth from working people to financiers or to capitalists.

I see no value in a system in which rules and borders are removed so that a few people are able to manipulate the financial system to steal the wealth of society. We end up with a society divided between billionaires on the one hand and people trying to live on a dollar a day on the other. That is just not acceptable. The alternative to the global capitalist system is radical democracy and truly democratic political institutions based on one person, one vote — not one dollar, one vote.

A real market economy operates within a framework of rules, distributes economic power and assets, and creates an ethical culture that nurtures a sense of mutual responsibility, not only to one another but also to the living systems of the Earth. Real markets are places where people are involved in productive exchange, with a mindfulness of their own needs and those of the larger community in which they live.

Mindful enterprises are owned by real people who are (at the same time) entrepreneurs, workers, managers, and community members. Their businesses are small and local: farms, health food stores, bakeries, services, convenience stores, hardware stores, and community bookstores. These can be family owned, worker owned, community owned, or owned as consumer cooperatives. They function within a framework of values and culture. Agreed-upon rules require that they absorb their costs, pay fair wages, pay attention to environmental and sustainable needs, and so forth.

In a real market economy, people realize that they need a livelihood. To create one, they come up with goods or services that they can provide to others in their community. Thus, they create a thriving, self-organizing local economy.

Real market economies also distribute property relatively equitably. I think private property is a wonderful thing. It's so good that everybody should have some! In fact, it should be an ownership stake in the means of creating your livelihood: this follows the argument of English philosopher John Locke, who established the intellectual legitimacy of property rights. Looking at the development of a society during its frontier era, Locke argued that when a person goes out and clears a piece of land to grow food for themselves and their family, they acquire a right to it because they have made it productive. (His argument was based on the assumption that there is sufficient land available for other people to clear for their livelihoods, too.) Since there are limits to the amount of land that one individual could clear, acquisition is naturally regulated. Distributed thusly, property rights serve to root economic and political power in the citizenry, as a counter to the potential abuse of state power, and provide the foundation for strong and prosperous democratic societies.

It is very different in a world in which the net worth of the world's 358 billionaires roughly equals the aggregate annual incomes of the world's 2.5 billion poorest people. Under conditions of extreme inequality, property rights and living rights come into conflict, and the free market becomes an instrument of tyranny rather than an agent of democracy.

The problem with global capitalism is the publicly traded, limited liability corporation. Its shares are sold freely in financial markets, by people who have no real connection to the firm and who bear no accountability for the corporation's actions. For the most part, owners of this kind of corporation don't even know what they own; their relationship is purely financial. The only thing they know about their portfolio is what kind of financial returns are being produced. There is no accountability or even knowledge of the social or environmental consequences of what the corporation is doing. Add to that a limited liability, so that there's no legal liability on the part of the shareholder for anything beyond, at maximum, the value of their shares. (Limited liability also tends to protect managers who are simply acting on behalf of shareholders who bear no particular responsibility.) You end up with an institutional form that, by design, concentrates power without accountability. (Some refer to it as a system of organized irresponsibility.) Now, if you also don't have strong antitrust laws, the limited liability corporation becomes a vehicle for concentrating wealth without limit and in perpetuity. Because, unlike people who die at some point, there is no limitation on the life of a corporation.

If we want to create just, sustainable, and compassionate societies, is there any proper role for an institution that concentrates power without accountability and without limit? I don't think so. It is wholly contrary to our democratic values. It is, in some ways, even contrary to the institution of monarchy, because at least there is the presumption that a monarch is supposed to rule in the interests of the whole. There is no such presumption for a corporation: it is only

ANOTHER VOICE

A commercial world, a corporate world, is not the natural state of things, even though corporations and the media would have us believe that. If it was the natural state, we wouldn't need to be constantly bombarded with advertisements.

— Nell Geizer

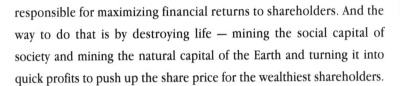

responsible for maximizing financial returns to shareholders. And the way to do that is by destroying life — mining the social capital of society and mining the natural capital of the Earth and turning it into quick profits to push up the share price for the wealthiest shareholders.

So, what can we do? The most immediate agenda is radical reform of the political system, the electoral system. We need to get bribery out of politics. We need campaign finance reform. We need to bring integrity into the electoral process. Also, we must open up the system to third-party voices, through proportional representation, instant runoff voting, and the opening up of debates.

We need to develop a cultural consciousness and wake up to the distinctions between reality and what the culture teaches us about the proper relationship between races and genders, between people and the environment, between people and the economy, and so forth.

We also need to rediscover our spiritual foundation. Western science has created a focus on materialism and mechanics, to the exclusion of spirit, and the development of a capitalist system plays into a materialist, consumerist culture. Together, these alienate us from our own spiritual nature and from the reality of the spiritual interconnections of life. When we break out of that alienation and discover life's inherent interconnection, it completely changes our concept of ourselves and allows us to find sources of energy and creativity that are otherwise blocked.

We still need political strategies, but they must be chosen to advance the cultural awakening. When there are sufficient numbers of people in a culturally awakened state, we'll be able to mobilize the political energy necessary to bring about changes of the magnitude discussed.

David Korten is the founder of People-Centered Development Forum; he is also cofounder and the board chair of the Positive Futures Network — publishers of Yes! A Journal of Positive Futures. *David is the author of* When Corporations Rule the World, *and* The Post Corporate World.

LINKS

www.futurenet.org
www.yesmagazine.org

▶ 47.

Interfaith Action
Bringing Spirit into Social Change

| EBOO PATEL |

My grandmother in Bombay sings in the morning and watches Hindi films. She feeds me nonstop and tells me reading will ruin my eyes. Pretty typical for an Indian grandmother. About three weeks in to my last trip to Bombay, I woke up and found a new person sitting on the sofa. She was barefoot and wearing a torn white nightgown a few sizes too large for her. Probably not a house-guest, I thought.

"Who is she?" I asked my grandmother.

"Call her Anisa. I don't know her real name," she told me.

"What is she doing here?" I asked.

"Her father and uncle beat her, so she has come here. We will keep her safe. Now don't answer the door for the next few days. Her father and uncle are probably angry, and they might come looking for her."

My grandmother has been sheltering abused woman for 40 years by hiding them in her home. Those who are interested in education, she sends to school. Those who want to go live with family in another part of India, she pays travel money to. Others just stay until they get married and start families. My grandmother has pictures of some of them, faded black and white shots, with scribbles on the back telling the story.

KAREN YOSHIKO MATSUOKA

▲

Eboo Patel

| 209 |

After hearing the stories of 10 or 12 of these women, I wanted to know one more story — my grandmother's.

"Why do you do this?" I asked.

"Because I'm a Muslim. This is what Muslims do," she said.

Amazing how one incident, one sentence, can make things suddenly clear. I had been doing social justice work since I was 17 — trying to save a homeless shelter in my college town, teaching in the ghettoes of Chicago, and protesting against the death penalty. I read Noam Chomsky and Karl Marx and raged against the machine. The drops of anger in me were constantly on the boil. But what happens when they evaporate? Will my commitment go as well? My grandmother's comment about being a Muslim touched on the ocean of love within me. "The true revolutionary," said Che Guevara, "is motivated by great quantities of love."

I read Islam as the story of prophets and poets who sought to create a more just Earth. Muhammad's first message to the people in Mecca was *tazaqqa* — compassion and generosity. He told them to treat the beggar, the orphan, and the widow — the most marginalized of Meccan society — with kindness and justice.

Fourteen hundred years later, the Indian Muslim philosopher, Muhammad Iqbal wrote, "Action is the highest form of contemplation." The true radical Islam is not Khomeini's death sentence on Salman Rushdie nor the terrorism of Osama Bin Laden but the South African Muslim, Farid Esack's insistence that Muslims be committed to social justice, individual liberty, and the quest for the Transcendent, who is beyond all institutional religious and dogmatic constructions.

T.S. Eliot wrote that we do not simply inherit traditions, we must work to belong to them. This is my challenge. Being a Muslim is a daily activity. Through prayer, reflection and action I cultivate what Muslims call *taqwa*— God consciousness. *Taqwa* anchors and guides me. Touching base with my *taqwa* reminds me that justice is deeply embedded in the nature of the universe, and it is our job to try to realize it on Earth.

My brothers and sisters on this path are Jews, Hindus, Christians, Buddhists, and Muslims who also get clarity, conviction, and courage from their faith. I am constantly amazed by how much we have in common. As I cultivate my *taqwa*, my Buddhist friends work on their Buddha nature, my Hindu friends seek to realize their *Atman*, and my Christian friends quote from the Social Gospel. When I describe my commitment to justice and generosity, my Jewish friends point me to a similar concept in their tradition, called *tzedaqa*.

Interfaith consciousness is not new. Gandhi borrowed the concept of nonviolence from Jainism and learned about the Christian Social Gospel through reading Tolstoy. He mixed this together with his Hindu faith and fashioned *satyagraha* — truth force, the spirit of the movement that liberated India. Howard Thurman and Martin Luther King, Jr. interpreted *satyagraha* within their own traditions and applied them to the American South during segregation. The Dalai Lama and the Sri Lankan leader Dr. A.T. Ariaratne are currently using the work of Gandhi, Thurman, and King in their own Buddhist way. Imagine if these people could have worked together. This is the opportunity of our day. Technology and diversity allow us to have conversations and create networks we could not have dreamed of 50 years ago. Creativity emerges in this dialogue and cooperative action follows.

Allah breathed his spirit into humanity and commissioned us to be his *Abd* and *Khalifa* — his servant and representative on Earth. My grandmother takes this responsibility seriously. I have brought

Jewish, Christian, Buddhist, and Hindu friends to meet with her. She asks them what they are doing to make the world a better place, closes her eyes in prayer when they sing sacred songs from their traditions, and blesses us when we leave on interfaith projects. One night, after dinner, she said to me, "You children, your hearts are with God." My grandmother sees it — we are a blessed generation. We will be remembered as the ones who brought Creation in line with the original vision of the Creator.

Eboo Patel is the executive director of the Interfaith Youth Corps. He is a Rhodes Scholar completing a Doctorate in the Sociology of Religion at Oxford University. Eboo has worked as a teacher, organizer, and writer on four continents.

LINKS

www.ifyc.org

▶ 48.

Dishonor Killings
Horrific Crimes Against Women

| DR. RIFFAT HASSAN |

There are two myths that you find in the Jewish, Christian, and Islamic traditions upon which rest the idea that men are superior to women. These ideas are that God's primary creation was Adam and from the rib of this male person, God created a woman — secondary and subordinate to man. The second is that although she's secondary in creation, she got Adam thrown out of paradise. Therefore women are to be seen as temptresses and seductresses, weak and dangerous to men.

I've done a lot of theological work to show that these beliefs are not supported by the basic teachings of Islam. The average Muslim thinks that woman was created from Adam's rib, but this story is not found in the *Qu'ran*, the sacred book of the Muslims. It has infiltrated into the Islamic tradition. In the *Qu'ran* there are 30 creation passages in which it says that God created all human beings at the same time and in the same manner. This shows that the traditional beliefs about women are contrary to *Qu'ranic* teaching.

In Pakistan, as in other cultures, honor is very prized by males. If a woman is seen by men as somehow compromising herself, then men believe they have the right to take that woman's life. A

▲

Dr. Riffat Hassan

woman can bring shame on her family through allegations of an illicit affair or rape, for marrying a man of her choice, or for the merest rumor of impropriety. Basically, the idea is that women belong to men as property, and if a woman causes them to lose face in society, the men can kill her. These are called honor killings.

According to Amnesty International, an average of two women each day are killed in Pakistan for betraying the honor of a husband or family. An honor killing is the easiest way for a man to get rid of his wife. But we know that a lot of these crimes are camouflage for other crimes. Amnesty International, for instance, recorded a case where a man had a quarrel with another man and killed him. In order to cover up his crime, he killed his sister-in-law and then made it look like an honor killing. He got away with it because honor killings are not regarded as crimes; nobody takes them seriously. There was also a very famous case last year (2000) in Pakistan, where a young woman was killed in a lawyer's office at the instigation of her parents because she wanted a divorce from her very abusive husband. The case became so politicized that the matter went to the Pakistani parliament. A group of senators wanted to discuss it, but in the end it was drowned out, because people said there's no discussion on matters of honor.

The problem with honor crimes and honor killings is that, because these are crimes committed by family members, most remain hidden. The police are very prejudiced against women, so they don't report or record the crimes. And the courts don't do anything about it.

But, there's a growing movement against honor killings. Women's groups, young Muslims and Pakistanis (especially in the West), mainstream Muslims, liberal, progressive Muslims, and a lot of men are protesting it. When they see graphic images of the women who are being burned, mutilated, and murdered, they feel that they have to do something. They want people to know that the stereotype of Muslims as terrorists or extremists is wrong. The vast majority, more than 90 percent of Muslims, are mainstream. They want to be modern; they want to have human rights.

Pakistan now has a military government. General Musharraf has made a statement that honor killings have no place in Islam and in law and should be very severely denounced. So that's a hopeful statement. It has taken a lot of effort to get him to make that statement — effort and educational campaigns. That must continue, if we are to see our government implement some serious changes and help us put an end to this horror.

Dr. Riffat Hassan is the director of the International Network for the Rights of Female Victims of Violence in Pakistan, which works to create a heightened awareness worldwide of the degree and nature of violence towards girls and women in Pakistan and to examine the root causes.

LINKS

www.inrfvvp.org

▶ 49.

Women's Empowerment
Deep Awareness Education

| COUMBA TOURÉ |

Coumba Touré

I've taken a strong stand for women, because I have witnessed a lot of abuse done to women by men and by other women based on a system of belief or tradition. Whether it's cultural or imported, or whether it comes from the colonizer, I see it as very oppressive. First, I had to start fighting for myself in my own family, just to survive and to make sure my rights were respected, before I could fight for anyone else.

My work on behalf of women's empowerment began when I heard about a woman named Doki Niasse from Senegal, who was beaten to death by her husband. I don't remember the year but I was pretty young. When I heard what happened, it hit me. I always knew something was wrong, but I couldn't really put it into words. To see the story out in the newspaper and to see that someone had taken a stand for her was such an eye opener. It gave me a space to express my anger. Not just about that beating, but about all of the injustices I could see against women.

I remember campaigning in Dakar. I put posters up about what happened to her, told people her story. All I cared about was finding out how to make sure the same thing didn't happen to us. I was trying to figure out how to educate young women so that they didn't have to feel like they're slaves attached to somebody who has a better economic status; to empower them to know who they are, so that they don't feel that just because they're women they're less and need to be silent. I just went on a quest to find out how I could reach them.

The campaign for Doki Niasse was not successful as far as the campaign itself went. The husband was arrested but then released, because he was powerful and part of a big religious family — after the whole mobilization, after all we did to make it public, no one really took it seriously. But it did give me a sense that I could do something. It didn't matter to me whether we won that battle. I mean, it was hard to take that he just got out of jail so easily: how can people be so unjust? But at the same time, it opened my eyes. I realized that I could do these kinds of things for other causes, and I learned how to be ready and better prepared.

My work on the Doki Niasse campaign also showed me just how much women were oppressed. It was no longer just her husband I was angry with or trying to oppose. I realized he was only able to beat her and kill her because he had a lot of cultural support to do it. If he went on trial and was acquitted and didn't even have to stay in jail, it was like: Wow, it's much more than him. And that told me there were a lot of things to do; it gave me a sense that what I had to struggle with is so large and so big. So I kept on doing it.

The one thing that I could call a success story — which motivated me to go further in this work — was the case of a woman in Chad. Her name is Zarah Yacoub. She produced a small video on female genital mutilation that won an international prize. When they showed the movie to the Imam and his followers, she got a *fatwa* (a sentence issued by a religious authority, the severity of which varies from case to case) against her. She was banned from her country and had a death sentence on her head. Some Muslims (but by no means all) believe that female genital mutilation is a way to keep women's sexuality in line; anybody opposing or attacking that is attacking the fundamentals of what they believe. So, she was in danger of being hurt or even being killed. (The practice of female genital mutilation is not rooted in Islam; it is also practiced by other religious groups, including some Christians.)

I was working for a woman's network in Senegal, and I saw this little blurb in the newspaper — a tiny paragraph telling about this *fatwa* against Zarah Yacoub. It was so small I hardly noticed it. So we were like: We need to do something. I said, "Why don't we build an international alert around it?" So we did. And it worked, because people were calling all the time and sending letters. They just swamped the whole government, writing to the President, to the Minister of Justice, to the police department. It was just amazing. I really didn't expect anything spectacular to happen, but the President of Chad called the Imam and told him he had to take back the *fatwa*. I was so happy when I heard about it.

Although I have never met Zarah, I talked with her on the phone when the *fatwa* was taken back. She was so happy. She wrote letters thanking me, and I was like: Wow, this can really work. It gave me a lot of courage. I don't think I'll ever doubt for one second. Even if there's only one chance that something can work, I'll try it, because it was so powerful to see that we could win.

ANOTHER **VOICE**

Feminism isn't spoken everywhere; in fact, you rarely hear even its whisper. After years of complacency, youth are once again rising against the forces of oppression, yet gender remains a territory uncovered in protests and demonstrations. If activists do mention women's issues, it is largely under the guise of a grander issue like globalization. But feminism deserves a voice at the roundtable of dispute, because patriarchy is very much in place, and women face strong sexism across cultural, ethnic, economic, and racial boundaries.

— Ali Pearson

After that, I left Dakar and went to Mali. I realized that I needed to be creating something new, that I couldn't just keep on fighting what exists. I couldn't just be reacting all the time to what was happening. I had to find a way to get something else started in the midst of the craziness; for me that was popular education. It gave me hope. You can really start from scratch. You can do deep awareness raising with people and believe that, in time, they'll be a strong group of people who will rise to what has to be worked on and changed.

Going to the 1995 Women's World Conference in Beijing also strengthened me. I met so many women there who were doing so many things. Knowing that I was not alone helped me to feel a sense of completion. It was like: I can do anything because I'm ready to fight and campaign even if I fail. And I'm ready to look for tools that will work. I'm also ready to be connected with people that are doing the same work. It was like coming full circle.

Daughters Sisters Project, girls' international focus group, Beijing 1995

I had crazy stories on my way to Beijing. I got locked up in jail for 24 hours. That was another eye-opening experience for me, another piece of struggle that was not a woman's struggle but a poor people's struggle. Before I left Mali, I got a visa to go to Beijing

Coumba Touré is the founder of Siggil Afrique *(meaning "heads up"), in Dakar, Senegal. She writes, "Every stand I take, I give thanks to my sisters and to those who believe in me and lift me up by trusting me with their lives: Suzanne, Maria, Debbie, Seynabou, Ayesha, and Rose."*

through Spain and France, but the French wouldn't give me a transit visa. I wouldn't stop my travel, so I was arrested in Spain. I went through the craziest time with the police, with them not understanding me and totally disrespecting who I was. It was really an interesting negotiation for me to get out of jail. Thanks to a group of women who supported me, I made it to Beijing.

From that jail experience, I got lessons, especially about holding on to who I am. I remember on that plane ride to France talking to a woman sitting right next to me. She was Spanish and was really nice, explaining what she was doing, talking to me about her child and everything.

Now, I'm somebody who is very outgoing, and I was talking to her but I wasn't really there. All these things that went on were on my mind. I was kind of automatically answering her questions. And then after a moment, I kind of woke up and I was like: Whoa! And I looked at the woman and I thought: I'm so tired, should I even be talking to her? Maybe I should just tell her I don't really want to discuss anything. But I was like: This is not fundamentally who I am. I was still curious about who she was.

In my heart I was like: Okay Coumba, if from here you change your fundamental nature, it really means that they killed something in you in that jail. That's the most important thing you need to hold on to. Let that experience make you firm in who you were before you got there. That moment was a big revelation to me, and I keep it as a reference point to my activism. On top of trying to change things, fighting, and standing for a lot of things, it was an integration about who I was and about how I relate to people. And it was about how to hold on to that no matter what's going on. It was a real defining point.

▶ 50.

Not Guilty

Speaking Truth to Power

| BETTY KRAWCZYK |

▲

Betty Krawczyk

O n January 25, 2001, 'Grandma K' Betty Krawczyk was freed
after serving four months of a year-long sentence imposed upon
her for her actions in blockading logging roads in the Elaho
*Valley of Canada. Her trial judge justified the lengthy sentence as
due to her criminal contempt. Vancouver judges Donald and
McKenzie overturned the sentence.*

What follows are excerpts from the transcript of her
*original sentencing hearing. Krawczyk is responding to a challenge
from the judge, who has asked her to explain why she blocked a
road and why she doesn't respect the law.*

"... I hear so often from friends and people who love me,
'Why do you do this? It's not called for. Let things work out as they
will,' but if everybody did that, the society would never evolve. We
wouldn't get anywhere, ever. I know the difference between
lawlessness and responsibility, and the only way things ever change
is through responsibility and the willingness to take on the
consequences of the actions when one is trying to make change. It's
just that it strikes a point with me because my little granddaughter
says, 'Grandma, why don't you leave those trees alone and come play
with me?' She doesn't understand it, either.

| 221 |

"About sentencing, specifically my own sentencing. Sir, I can only say that I am responsible for my own actions. The devil didn't make me blockade Interfor logging trucks, and God didn't make me do it either. Neither did PATH [People's Action for Threatened Habitat] or FAN [Forest Action Network] or Friends of the Elaho. I told me to do it.

"In my opinion, my attempt to try to help stop Interfor's rapid destruction of the Elaho Valley by standing in front of the logging trucks was not an evil, criminal, crazy thing to do. In my scheme of things, it was the eminently sane thing to do. I believe it to be crazy and insane to stand by mutely while our collective life-support systems are being destroyed.

"I do not regret my actions in the slightest. And when I am in jail I consider myself a political prisoner and I act accordingly. But, in reality, the only real freedom that anyone actually finds is with the confines of one's own mind and spirit. It sounds trite, I know, but that kind of freedom really can't be imprisoned.

"You can put me in jail, sir, but I will not be your prisoner. I will not be Interfor's prisoner, or a prisoner of the Attorney General, or a prisoner of these nice deputy sheriffs, or a prisoner of BCCW [Burnaby Correctional Centre for Women]. I am only a prisoner of my own conscience, sir, and that makes me a free woman, a free person.

"And, as a free person, I refuse to enter into any sort of collusion with this court in terms of potential house arrest or electronic monitoring as part of my sentence. I will never be a party to assisting in my own punishment in ways that would force me to internalize prison, to internalize confinement, to internalize guilt, to internalize the power of Interfor and the Attorney General's office to punish me for trying to protect public property, property that every citizen has a right to, not only a right but also a duty to protect and enjoy and love.

"As well, sir, I will not accept any kind of community service as part of punishment. I have done more than my share of community service in my lifetime. I have done it freely and as a labor of love, and I will not have it imposed on me as punishment. I will also resist paying a fine, however small. To pay a fine, at least for me, would be tantamount to admitting guilt. This would imply that my actions in the Elaho were harmful and antisocial and must be atoned for. And again if I pay the fine, however small, I would have to internalize a sense of guilt that I do not feel.

"There have been actions in my life that I truly regret and feel sorry for, but trying to protect the ancient forest of the Elaho is not one of them. I love the Elaho. I love all of the old-growth forests of British Columbia. To fight to preserve what one loves is to act in harmony with oneself and with nature.

"So, sir, I refuse anything that would dilute the reasons of why I am here, of why I tried to stop the logging of the Elaho. I refuse fines, community service, and the internalized guilt of a shamed and shameful compliance. You must lock me up, sir, or let me go. Thank you."

Born and raised in the bayous of Southern Louisiana, Betty Krawczyk is the mother of eight children, an equal number of grandchildren, and a great-grandchild. She has spent her entire life engaging in social issues, dating back to the Civil Rights struggles in her home state, and she was cofounder of one of the first women's centers in Canada.

▶ 51.

Surviving the Storm
Lessons from Nature

| JULIA BUTTERFLY HILL |

Julia Butterfly Hill

I didn't come from a background of activism, but when I first saw what was happening to the ancient redwoods in California, I fell to the ground and started crying and immediately got involved. It changed my life. Everyone thinks, when they hear I'm the poster child of tree huggers, that I must be a hard-core radical extremist, whacko, granola-munching, you name it — all in capital letters, with quotes. But, I was just dumped in the deep end of the entire movement — not just tree-sitting, not just forest issues, but the whole social, environmental, and consciousness movement — and said to myself: Better swim or you're going to drown! So I started learning how to swim.

Along the way I learned: by watching and talking, by asking questions, and by listening over and over during the 738 days that I sat in the ancient spreading branches of Luna. I saw how each different tactic is used and why it's being used. I realized that the best tools for dismantling the machine are the ones the mechanics are using to keep it running. I saw very early on that the mechanics in this situation are corporations, corporate media, and the government — all in a kind of collusion together. They say only a little bit, and usually a majority of what they say is skewed so that the participant on the other end (whether they're watching, listening, or reading) doesn't get the truth. And if you don't have the truth, then you cannot make an informed decision. And if you don't have an informed decision, then you cannot take a conscious act. And if you do not take a conscious act, then you're part of the annihilation of the gift of life, period.

I saw that some of the tactics activists were using were not working, because they weren't using the tools of the mechanic. They were going out there and sitting in trees. They were getting beaten up, killed, or thrown into jail with ridiculous charges by cops who pepper sprayed them. But nobody except the local community knew they were out there.

SHAUN WALKER

It was kind of like preaching to the choir. And we need to do that to inspire. I spend a lot of time preaching to the already converted because it hurts to care in today's world. It's easy to go numb and tune it out, whether you're 15, 25, or 50. But we still need to care, and to do that we need truth and inspiration, information and hope — that gives us the tools to take conscious actions toward positive change. At the same time, though, we must utilize the tools of the mechanics (who are trying to keep the machine running) in order to take it down. Otherwise, it's like trying to use a hammer to turn a screw.

I was in a situation with Luna where I had to learn to listen to nature and respect it, or die. My life was on such a precipice the entire time I was up there. It was just really fragile in so many ways. The first three months were so hard that I was praying to die. I didn't want to hurt that bad anymore. And yet at the same time I didn't want to give up. But, when death did start to come, I started praying for life. I was constantly on this emotional roller coaster — spiritually and physically. It was one assault after the other.

One day, they were cutting down trees all around me, and I started crying and hugging Luna. I was crying because I felt ashamed to be in white skin. I felt ashamed to be part of a race of people who perpetuated genocide thousands of years ago and have now made it our mission to perpetuate genocide on the rest of the planet and life in all its forms. It was eating me alive from the inside out. I was so angry and so hurt and ashamed, and I held onto Luna and was crying and apologizing over and over, saying: I'm so sorry. I'm so sorry.

When I finally sat up, I realized I was covered in sap. Climbing around in Luna before, I had gotten a little bit of sap on me, but I had never been covered like I was this day. I realized that sap was pouring out from all over her, actually pouring. I could see the sap flowing, which I had never really seen before, and it hit me: this was Luna communicating her grief. Sap is just like grief. It's not something you can wash away; it clings to you and becomes a part of who you are. And it was then that I realized nature was communicating to me. (Later on, people sent me scientific proof that sap is one of the ways trees communicate!)

I started paying attention. I started listening and getting answers from everything — from Luna, the birds, the bears, the shapes of the pine needles. Everything became my teacher when I opened up. My relationship with Luna grew. I realized that Luna has been communicating with humankind for 1,000 years, and we just forgot how to listen. But I learned how to listen, and from that moment on everything started coming to me. Sometimes, I'd have to get beaten over the head a little bit before I'd go: Oh yeah, thank you. What are you trying to tell me? My connection with Luna and my connection with nature is what kept me going, kept me alive, helped teach me the vital lessons I needed to learn when I was about to give up or make a very big mistake. I'm forever thankful for that.

One of the lessons I learned and something that I use a lot now is how to survive a storm. I nearly died up there, in the worst winter storms recorded in the history of California. The trees taught me that the way to make it through those storms (and the storms of life) is to stay rooted and centered but not rigid. The trees and branches that try too hard to stand strong and straight are the ones that break. The only ones that make it through are the ones that know to bend and flow and let go. So, I've been using that now in my life. I use it when I'm being barraged by the media, by grassroots activists, by mainstream community, by everything. I just bend and flow when I see the wind coming; I loosen up and get ready to get blown, and then I kind of flex back into place. And I'm ready to get up the next morning and do it all over again.

The legacy that I left behind was a vision of a better world. We protected a grove of old-growth forest. And we left a living embodiment of what that vision of a better world is all about: a world where the last of our ancient and old-growth forests and wild

ANOTHER **VOICE**

When a human being acts in accordance with her or his innermost principles, that person is very powerful. Almost invincible. There is great power when you have no doubt or conflict with what you are doing. We must discover our real, basic values, because once we are working within those values, nothing can stop us.

— Severn Cullis-Suzuki

Julia Butterfly Hill is a writer, poet, activist, and cofounder of The Circle of Life Foundation. She is known worldwide for her courageous two-year tree-sit atop Luna, a 180-foot-high (55-meter-high), 1,000-year-old redwood tree in Humboldt County, California.

LINKS

www.circleofllifefoundation.org
www.ottermedia.com

places are protected. A world where the watersheds we're all a part of are protected, even if we live in LA, Chicago, Detroit, or New York City. All those places that look nothing like nature anymore are actually a part of a watershed, and that watershed is the nature that beats its pulse underneath the asphalt and the concrete and steel. That watershed is our lifeblood, what keeps us alive.

To live a life of service for a better world is a legacy that doesn't disappear. It's an imprint, and that imprint can be negative or positive, depending upon the actions and choices we make every single moment of every single day. I have to tell you the coolest people I've ever met, young and old, are the ones who are out there giving their life for a good cause. They glow more; they're the most beautiful, magnificent, powerful people I've ever seen. They're much more powerful than the richest person and more beautiful than any model, because their beauty and power resonates from deep within the life force all the way through their body, and shines out. I've never wanted to kneel in front of a model or an actor or actress or a corporate billionaire, but I want to bow myself before people who are activists or who work for the common good. That's honor. Money is not honor. Doing something of real value with one's life is honor.

▶ 52.

One Million Postcards
Remember the Iraqi Children

| KOUTHAR AND MARWA AL-RAWI |

▲

*Kouthar and Marwa Al-Rawi
with Iraqi children.*

Some say it takes a village to raise a child. My sister and I disagree. We believe it takes a world to raise a child. Unfortunately, many villages today do not work together or get along. They bomb, murder, terrorize, and blackmail each other behind closed doors and in the public eye. Villages pass policies (like sanctions) on each other, which harm children and take away basic human rights.

My sister and I decided to take responsibility for the world we live in. Our work starts with our village, the United States, and its policy of sanctions against other villages, countries, and nations. The US imposes unilateral sanctions against some 75 countries, most notably against Cuba. The list goes on to include Iran, Libya, North Korea, and Sudan, just to name a few. The US also supports multilateral sanctions with other nations against Angola, Liberia, Rwanda, and Somalia. And finally the village under the severest sanctions of all — Iraq.

On August 6, 1990 the UN Security Council adopted Resolution 661, imposing economic sanctions and a full trade embargo on Iraq. Those sanctions deny the children adequate food, clean water, and medicine. According to the United Nations International Children's Fund (UNICEF), the sanctions cause 5,000 deaths of children under the age of

Kouthar Al-Rawi

five each month. This has gone on for ten years and has killed more than half a million children.

The charter of the United Nations says, "We the people of the United Nations are determined to save succeeding generations from the scourge of war." Why then are the children in Iraq not being saved? Are they different from the children of all the villages that make up the world?

With the belief that one person can change the world, and knowing that human rights make our world a more decent place to live, my sister and I started a campaign called "Remember the Iraqi Children," in January 1998. We started our campaign with $82.00 from garage sales and the recycling of cans. We work hard every day for the smallest opportunities, so that even one more person can be educated about the sanctions and join our campaign. We write letters and articles for magazines and newspapers, give lectures, and go to protests. One organization financed our video about our campaign and about how to grassroots organize. In 1999, it won the Liv Ullman Peace Prize at the Chicago International Children's Film Festival. That year, we also traveled to Geneva, Switzerland and gave speeches at the United Nations Roundtable "The Art of Making Peace." And we have traveled to Iraq on three occasions to witness and document what the sanctions are doing to the Iraqi children.

Today, the UN General Assembly and Security Council have realized that the sanctions have been a failure. If given a chance, they would repeal the sanctions. However, the United States and Britain continue to support and sustain these terrible sanctions. The US president has the power to end the sanctions today.

Our goal is to collect one million postcards from around the world from adults and children, protesting the sanctions on Iraq for the sake of the children. The postcard can be drawn, or a poem or message written to the US President asking him to lift the sanctions. We are organizing the postcards into one of the most important art shows the world will ever see. We ask the question: What is the most important artwork or messages in the world? We believe it is the artwork or message that can save the life of a child.

We hope all of these cards will convince the US President to lift the sanctions on Iraq. We hope that the cards will educate other people against sanctions and let them know these acts only hurt the weak in any village (especially the children). A village under sanctions cannot raise a child.

My sister and I started this campaign not knowing what a huge impact it would have on our lives. In the beginning, it took every waking moment to get the word out. We realized very early on that we were working against an almost total media block concerning the sanctions. And when it is reported on, it is not truthful and is often misleading. This work (campaign) is our life. We now sneak in soccer and a few acting classes here and there for fun, but we know it is going to be a long, continuous struggle to get the sanctions lifted. And then, when the Iraqi sanctions are lifted, our work will still not be done, because the children in Sierra Leone and Palestine will need our help.

Send postcards to:

One Million Postcards to the President Campaign,

PO Box 1141, San Pedro, California 90733, USA

Marwa Al-Rawi is an eighth grade student at Dodson Magnet Middle School. She plays on a soccer team and hopes to go into the medical profession. Kouthar Al-Rawi is in the ninth grade at San Pedro High School and plays on its soccer team. She hopes one day to be an architect. Both Marwa and Kouthar devote their spare time to their campaign.

LINKS

www.iraqikids.com

▶ 53.

Ban Landmines
A Young Survivor Speaks Out for Peace

| SONG KOSAL |

COURTESY OF MINES ACTION CANADA/ACTION MINES CANADA

▲

Song Kosal

I am very lucky to have belonged to The Campaign to Ban Landmines since I was 12 years old. I went to Vienna, Austria in 1995 to call for a total ban on landmines for helping the children to run and play freely without fear. On March 8, 2001, I spoke in Washington, DC outside the Capitol Building and asked the United States government to ban landmines.

Having lost a leg from a landmine, I am committed to stopping any further use of landmines. I told the government that my parents are farmers. They are poor and have seven children. I am the fourth in the family. Every day, I used to help take care of my young sisters and brother, as well as to do some other farming work. I want every child to be able to wear two shoes. In my country I asked a shoemaker to just make me one shoe. He said, "No! To make one shoe brings bad luck." I ask all the countries of the world to give the children of the future good luck — by banning landmines.

While standing on the UN podium and seeing many men in the big suits, I felt very afraid and forgot all the words that I wanted to say. I tried to look at my handicapped friends from Cambodia to help me. They made signs with their mouths to encourage me to speak out, but I was so nervous and could not articulate. The conference did not ban landmines.

Later, the Canadian government invited countries to come to Ottawa to sign the Mine Ban Treaty in December 1997, and I was there. Although not able to sign the government treaty, I was the first person to sign The Peoples' Treaty — a treaty where ordinary people promised to make sure their governments helped mine victims, funded mine clearance, and destroyed their stockpiles of mines.

I went to Ottawa, Canada in 1997 to make sure that the governments who signed the Mine Ban treaty would keep their promise in implementing it. In 1998, I attended the "Kids at War" meeting in Australia. I met Sandra, a handicapped girl from Angola (the one who regularly met with Princess Diana in calling for a total ban on landmines). Sandra and I decided to start a campaign called "Kids Against War". The treaty of the campaign is: "We want no more war; we want no more landmines; we want no more mine victims; and we will work for peace in our world."

The campaign grew. Mairead Corrigan and Adolfo Esquivel, two Nobel Peace Prize laureates, asked me and my friends: How are you going to work for peace? We thought about this. Then, one day, we were sitting near a pool of lotus flowers. The pink flowers were in blossom, and though water sat on the leaves and the petals, they never got wet. We asked ourselves: How can we live in a violent society and not get 'wet' from the violence?

We came up with a new call to youth and children everywhere, asking them to try to do five things to make the world a better place: Every day, I will do one thing to make peace grow like a flower. Every day, I will spend five minutes reflecting peacefully. I will help landmine survivors. I will care for and not destroy the environment. I will try to solve arguments without violence.

Song lost her leg when she was five years old. One year later, a landmine killed her older brother. When she's not campaigning against landmines, Song attends high school in Phnom Phen, Cambodia.

LINKS

www.icbl.org
www.minesactioncanada.org

▶ 54.

OTPOR!

The Student Movement to Overthrow Slobadan Milosevic

| NIKOLA DAMNJANOVIC - TRANSLATED FROM SERBIAN
  BY JANDRANKA MASIC |

In 1989, Slobadan Milosevic was elected president of Serbia. At that time, the economic situation in Belgrade was extraordinarily difficult. I was just a kid. My parents opposed Milosevic and raised me alike.

When I was 18 (in 1998), the OTPOR! (Resistance) Movement appeared for the first time in our town, Pancevo. I was in high school in Belgrade where OTPOR! started, so I knew a little about them. They were just an idea then, not an organization. Once they formed a group, they started doing protests, like spray-painting walls. They wanted fair and free elections, free university, and independent media. When the US started bombing Serbia, OTPOR! decided to take the organization to a higher level. They called together people that they could trust, and that was the moment when OTPOR! came into being in Pancevo in a formal sense.

Since we had no premises in which we could meet, the manager of the Youth Center gave us the keys so that we could meet every day. She had a lot of problems with people in the town because of that and endured a bunch of reproaches. In the beginning, we often met and talked for six or seven hours. At first, we had no

Nikola Damnjanovic

(second from left)

COURTESY OF NIKOLA DAMNJANOVIC

materials, no money, and it would have been illegal to register the organization, since we had members who were considered terrorists.

Our first action was against the opposition government of Slobadan Milosevic. We brought out on the street a red barrel with a picture of Milosevic on it, and everyone who wanted to kick the barrel had to pay something. With the money we collected, we printed the first fliers and posters. We had no brushes or buckets for the glue, but we worked in pairs and put the posters up anyway we could. There were only 10 of us in a town of 100,000. At that time, I was not afraid, just uncomfortable for my parents, who were worried. My best friend Steva and I would meet in the middle of the night to go put the posters up.

OTPOR!, as an organization, does not have a president, does not have a hierarchy. The status you achieve in OTPOR!, you achieve by your work. We have an application form, which is needed because we have to know on whom we can count, and some kind of administration has to exist. Anyone in OTPOR! can come up with a protest activity. If it appeals to everybody, then we work on it and we bring it into life.

The people in OTPOR! are of various ages, professions, and levels of education. Most are young, but there are also elders. We are all connected to the same idea, and we are all team players. Some people wanted to be part of OTPOR! after we gained recognition — mainly because they wanted to be photographed. And those who did not come did not want police to arrest and beat them.

Once we started to get attention, a complete reorganization notice was issued. OTPOR! was established in all the towns in Serbia, and we received the office in the Youth Center. The very next morning

the swastikas appeared on the door. Some people declared us domestic terrorists and foreign hirelings. We were getting materials from Belgrade, but there were hardly enough of them even for ourselves. We were lucky when we'd get enough buttons. The people in the organization divided into sections, and everyone did what they knew best. We had good marketing, and from that time on even bigger and bigger donations. The biggest donations were from our people in diaspora.

Many people were afraid of hired thugs. When I look back, I shudder at the danger I was in. When the police started to realize that we were a threat to them, some of us started to get taken to the police station to be interrogated. They thought that if they intimidated us, they would stop us. But what does not kill you makes you stronger.

The first one of us who got taken was Nenad Miletic. A few days later, the police came looking for me. They'd heard me speak at a protest at the local TV station the government wanted to close. The police went to my home and left an official summons, saying that they wanted to interrogate me at eight o'clock the next morning.

I went to the police station but not alone. We had called a lawyer and journalists, all from OTPOR! I was taken into a room and asked if I knew why I was there. I said that I supposed that I was there because of my participation with OTPOR! They said that it had nothing to do with that, that I was under suspicion of stealing a bike! At first, I laughed and then waited for them to start laughing, but they were serious. That was hilarious!

During the war, I stayed in my house in Pancevo. I did not think that anyone was crazy enough to shoot at civil targets — only the chemical and petrochemical targets. Most of my friends left, though. We lived normal lives (basketball matches and other things) and had a great time. Someone from outside here cannot comprehend this, but I was only afraid for my mom, because she was very frightened. We were wondering when it was all going to end.

We were angry, of course, with the Americans and at Europe. We felt there were other ways of solving things, besides bombing. The bombing only strengthened Milosevic's rule. Whenever we got a donation to OTPOR! from abroad, people would say that Clinton was giving us money, that we were getting money from the NATO aggressors who were killing our children.

In the media, we were called terrorists and hired spies. The government even tried to pass a terrorism law, where if you were caught and convicted, you'd get 40 years of prison. Luckily it didn't pass. That's when I started to get frightened and to think about the danger I was in. At that time, we started to hide all the administration material, all our supplies, and the names and application forms of all our members. That's when we started to work secretly.

Then my friend Nesa got beaten and the arrests began. Everyone got frightened, because we realized what was happening. We started passing information about meeting times and places in code. I was in charge of the material and was hiding it in the garage of our summer cottage, but there was not enough space. Also, we realized that we were being bugged. We had to take the batteries off our mobile phones, so that we could speak about where we would meet. We didn't tell anyone these things, except my dad, because he helped us drive around our materials. My mother was so afraid she could not sleep. She was sleeping on 3.2 tons of OTPOR! material; for just one sticker, she could have ended up in prison.

COURTESY OF NIKOLA DAMNJANOVIC

In Belgrade, a meeting of the opposition was organized. Two hundred and fifty of us set off from Novi Sad on foot, which is 53 miles (85 kilometers) away from Belgrade. At each town we entered along the way, at first everything was quiet and we did not know what to expect, but at the main square people welcomed us with food and song. It was the same with every place on our way to Belgrade. This gave us additional spirit. When we arrived in Belgrade, we got information that the police were waiting for us on the Branko Bridge, but that was disinformation. In fact, we were met by 100,000 people, many of whom offered us food and places to rest or sleep.

The elections were coming, so over the next days, we started putting up our posters and posters to help the opposition parties. It was a dangerous time. The police and hired thugs were cruising the town, finding people to beat. One night, my best friend Steva was beaten so badly he had to go to the emergency hospital. When I saw him, I was really shaken. Six or seven police had held him down and beaten him. I knew he was okay when he told me to go tell the girls he was a hero!

Then the fifth of October came, and we all went to Belgrade. That was the revolution about which everything is a known fact. Hundreds of thousands of people came into the streets, and many broke into the parliament building and the RTS station (state TV) and started fires. Finally, the police joined the protest. Everyone was demanding that Milosovic get out. He had lost the election earlier in the week. We knew he was through. We were so happy, we were like small children. For the first time we heard some normal news on TV.

I felt that I was participating in something very important, which gave me the opportunity not to stay just a number but to change the course of events.

We did a lot in one year. We did what the politicians could not have done or maybe did not know how to do. I think that we are still unconscious of all the things that were influenced by our work. We managed to wake people up from apathy, to break their habit of believing in everything that the state TV was telling them. But it's not over yet. We still have to have a complete reorganization of our system.

We influenced the process of cultural decontamination. Our help came from good people, who realized that we were fighting a good cause. For our work we received an international recognition when Branko Ilic and Milijana Jovanovoic got an award on MTV (Music Television). Then we realized how big our influence was on young people all over the world. I think we have shown that hate is not the way to change things; it's only with skillful diplomacy that we can try to do what is the best for us.

▼

Nikola Damnjanovic is a member of OTPOR!, the student resistance movement established in 1998, which grew from 15 students to a nation of people. With the financial aid of Western governments, principally the US, OTPOR! is credited with helping to overthrow former Serbian president, Slobadan Milosevic.

▶ 55.

The Courage to Protest
The Movement for Democracy in Sierra Leone

| STEVEN NABIEU ROGERS |

▲

Steven Nabieu Rogers

TUTALENI ASINO

Youth activism has been extremely dangerous in the small but troubled region of my home, Sierra Leone. Through my involvement in several student demonstrations and actions — amidst total chaos, political disorder, and violence — I have learned to endure and to follow what I believe.

It was common for students like me, who were struggling for democracy, to be marginalized and victimized by ambitious politicians. Having been a victim of police brutality and been forced many times to retract statements considered inimical by the government (with cigarette butts put out on our bodies), the suffering was always tolerated, as we were considered heroes when we emerged from those cells. But the incident I am about to explain stands unique from many of those arrests and temporary imprisonment. The circumstances that led me and a host of other youth to form the Movement for the Restoration of Democracy (MRD) were more serious than anything we'd ever seen before.

I was in my final year as an undergraduate in 1997, when the Armed Forces Revolutionary Council (AFRC) overthrew President Kabba's democratic government. Youth organizations took up the challenge to organize a peaceful protest against the junta (regime) — an undertaking that became the test of youth activism. As a member of the Student Union Government and the newly formed MRD, I coordinated a series of underground meetings to work out the details of the protest. These dangerous activities were done knowing that the junta was not recognized by the international community, that sanctions and starvation were affecting the country, and that nobody could come to the aid of the people apart from merely condemning what was happening.

The junta was determined to stay at all costs, including genocide, if that would consolidate them in power. The students of the MRD became targets and were to be 'silenced' if we were caught. Our only option was to flee the country or go underground. We went underground. Our mission: to uncover information about all AFRC secret killings and other atrocities and send it to a pirate radio station that was set up by the deposed civilian government as a propaganda machine.

After the AFRC was denounced on the BBC (the first denouncement from within Sierra Leone), the junta stepped up their actions, and we became the target of a manhunt. By then, the junta government was strangely united with the rebel movement. These rebels were notorious for hacking limbs with blunt machetes, splitting the stomachs of pregnant women, and burning human beings alive. They became the law enforcement agents for the AFRC.

The 18th day of August 1997 still haunts me. Against all odds, members of the MRD openly held a demonstration for the whole world to watch. Eight students were killed in cold blood. My friend Vafie Koneh was shot a few meters away from where I stood. Many others (me included) were arrested and taken to a road prison.

Strong images of those dark, stinky prison walls come back to me still. Not that I was a stranger there — I'd been arrested before — but this time there was blood all over the cell. The warden came and randomly collected two of our colleagues (one of whom was sitting right next to me), and I believe that I narrowly escaped death, because those two never came back.

I spent a month there, five days without food. Our colleagues were still on the campaign, which made matters worse for us. Every night, we were given 36 lashes — the scars on my hand are a constant reminder and a bitter legacy of those times. While I slept on the cold floor, I became more determined, knowing that our cause was for the majority of Sierra Leoneans.

My beliefs were eventually confirmed after the restoration of the democratic government in return for thousands of gallons of bloodshed. Today, no historian could write about my country without due regard to the MRD and the Student Union Government. The integrity of a nation was restored and belongs to us — the young generation. My friend Vafie Koneh and a host of others died, but their names will be remembered forever.

Steven Nabieu Rogers was 24 years old in 1997 when the Armed Forces Revolutionary Council (AFRC) took power in a bloody coup. He currently lives in Pennsylvania and works with Focus on Youth (FOY), an organization dedicated to the welfare of young people in Sierra Leone. Steven plans to return home to continue the work of helping his people.

▶ 56.

Brutal Exile
A Voice for the Refugees

| HARI ACHARYA |

Looking at the good side, I think I had a very, very positive childhood. But now as I reflect on it, I see that I grew up without knowing what was right and what was wrong. I grew up thinking I should do well in my studies, get a good degree, a good job, and make tons of money. The village I grew up in was so remote and primitive that you had to walk 12 hours from the nearest mud road to get there. We had no electricity and no market around us. I was in grade nine before I saw my first computer. We had no telephone services, no wireless, no images of the world. I'm not saying it was a bad childhood. I was happy.

In tenth grade, I experienced a shake-up in my consciousness and in my beliefs. The government of Bhutan had some benefits for students who did very well in their examinations: they would send one student to Canada and one to the United Kingdom. According to my understanding, that was supposed to be based on merit. I got second position in the country, which meant that I was 'in.' This was a big thing. Nobody had ever made it out to foreign countries from my block (a group of 10 to 12 neighboring villages). I was called for an interview along with 20 other students.

▲

Hari Acharya

| 243 |

The interview was given by the foreign minister and others from the National Council for the Promotion of Culture, and by the Director of Education. I was tested, and then they said to my face that I just didn't qualify.

Bhutan has three distinct cultures and, because I come from a culture that is practiced by the people in the south and not by the ruling monarchy, their feeling was that I would not be able to project Bhutanese culture to the western world. By then the government had come up with policies that said we were one nation and should be one people — which meant that you wear one dress; you follow one culture; you speak one language. They said it was to save ourselves against any foreign aggression, because we are a small country. So everybody had to follow the culture of the monarchy. It was then that I started thinking there was something totally wrong.

By 12th grade, I had this burning desire to try to change the system in Bhutan. I went to India in 1992 for a civil engineering course at West Bengal State, on a scholarship. This college had a totally different atmosphere. They had student unions with presidential elections and elections for the secretary general — things that didn't exist in my country.

After a month I had a vacation, and I was so excited to go home with all these wonderful ideas in my head. I could never have known what to expect when I arrived home. My dad was in jail because he and three of our friends had written a petition against the new village head man who had agreed to follow government policies that allowed him to throw people out of the country in exchange for compensation.

I had a long discussion with the man who locked up my father. I said, "My father has done the right thing. You are not supposed to lock him up for doing that. You should have investigated what was going on." We exchanged hard words. At one point his gun was at my temple and he said, "I'll blow your brains out if you don't shut up." I think at that point I was way beyond myself. So I said, "You can blow my brains out. I care more about justice and my father than my own brains. So you can go ahead." I don't know whether he had a bullet in there or not. He didn't do anything — but he locked me up next to my father.

Then they started torturing my father in the evening. They had been doing that for five days. Later, I found out that they would hang him upside down from the ceiling and then beat him until he started bleeding from the nose and the mouth. I could hear his cries for two days and after that I was totally traumatized. Of course, my dad was physically and mentally traumatized.

Finally, they took the two of us out of jail and brought us to an office, where they wanted my father to sign a form called the "Application to Leave the Country." It was a voluntary migration form that stated: "I, having listed the compensation for the property outlined above and taking all the family members outlined above, seek permission from the government of Bhutan to leave this country under my own will."

Surprisingly, after all that torture, my dad was still pretty strong. He wouldn't sign. Again they ordered him, and again they started kicking him with their boots, and thrusting the gun into his chest and his temple and his forehead. So I had this bright idea: What if we just sign it now and get out? We'll be back in a few months because the movement is building on all sides. People are supporting us. It's not necessary to take all this torture.

So my dad signed, and within ten days our house was locked up and we were out on the road. Twenty-three other families were expelled along with ours. It took us three days to reach the border, walking 12 hours each day.

When we got to the border, the district administration office stopped us. They wanted us to get some sort of permission from the district authority to get out of the country. First we were forced out and now they wouldn't let us go! We had to camp for 12 days at the riverbank — all 24 families. Each day, the head of each family would be called to the district administration office; they'd have to wait there the whole day. And they would come back in the evening, nothing having happened.

Maybe I would still have tried to embrace my origin and not gotten into activism, but on the seventh day of waiting at the border, 12 army guys came over to the camp when all the head men were gone. They pulled out three young women, all of whom were younger than me. I knew all of these gang rapes were going on, and I didn't want that to happen. So I shouted, "You have no right to take them. We know what you're going to do." Another boy my age joined me. We were all told to be quiet or otherwise they would shoot us.

They took us across the bend of the river to a big shed, where people from the north would come down in the winter and keep their cattle. No one was there. They stripped us boys naked and tied us to bamboo poles. Then they raped the three girls in front of us. That ordeal continued for one-and-a-half hours. I felt so, so, powerless. So cowardly. If I closed my eyes, they would hit me with the rifle butt and make me look at them. There was nothing I could do. When they left, the girls were just barely conscious. When they could, they untied us and we took them to the river. They washed themselves up and then we came back late in the evening.

The people in the camp didn't ask us anything. It was totally a passive acceptance of knowing that something horrible had happened and that there's nothing anyone can do to lessen the effect. That evening was so quiet. And I was still wondering why it had to happen, if we did something to provoke it. But there was nothing.

The next day, the district administrator came again with about 12 army guys and a video crew. He had a big bag of crisp, new bank notes. They wanted to take video interviews of people leaving the country under their own will. We had to smile, and we had to make gestures to show that we were happy and that nobody was forcing us to get out. If anybody refused, they would be told that whatever happened yesterday would happen again. It was then that I understood what that rape was all about. On that day, I made a decision: whatever happened — even if I couldn't take care of myself or my family — whatever it took, I would work for justice.

We finally made it to the refugee camp in Nepal, a very, very big camp that held 18,000 people. Eventually, we were transferred to a new camp that had no school, no good health facilities, and where all the new refugees were coming directly from Bhutan. These were traumatized people: kids who had recently been thrown out of school, people whose fathers were in jail or whose mothers had been raped.

Within about a month of reaching this new camp (where my family is still living), the Association of Human Rights Activists in Bhutan approached me. They asked me to help them document

COURTESY OF HARI ACHARYA

Girls in refugee camp

human rights violations that the people in the camps had undergone in Bhutan. They also wanted me to help them identify torture victims to determine whether or not they needed medical attention or counseling. So from 1993 to 1994, I worked as a teacher, documented human rights violations, and was a counselor for torture victims.

I used to go from hut to hut and talk to people. I'd write down their story, and if they had been tortured, I would get the details and their presenting symptoms. That really, really helped me. I found out that people had undergone much, much worse torture than my family and friends. It was some sort of healing experience for me. So many uneducated people had undergone so much, and they still survived and had so much hope of going back. I felt, as an educated person, I had something to offer and that I should help them and work for them. I continued until April 1994 in that capacity and was then given a scholarship by a program organized from Germany.

I went back to India for my graduation and got involved in the same kind of activism work that I had been doing. I was basically responsible for organizing the people in the Darjeeling area and getting them rallied behind our cause. I participated as an organizer in a peace march in 1996. We organized from the refugee camps in Nepal all the way to Bhutan — over 250 miles (400 kilometers).

We were supposed to arrive in Bhutan, talk with the king in person, and appeal to him, asking him to get the people back because they had been unjustly thrown out. But we were arrested in India and about 5,000 of our people went to jail. A group that we did get across to Bhutan was arrested, tortured, and deported.

Eventually, I joined a master's degree program in 1998. It was possible to go to school and be totally involved in the movement, so I made a tour of India and created new activist groups. Then in 1999, I came to the United States.

The terrible experiences that I have undergone have taught me a lot. Since being in the States, I have been involved in a youth action campaign for peace in Bhutan that has been organized by Global Youth Connect and an international human rights NGO based in New York. Through these programs, I have been going to colleges, universities, community groups, and high schools and talking to people about what's happening in the refugee camps and in Bhutan. I'm planning to stay here until I get my green card. I've been living on the good will of people — supporters and well wishers. My family supports my decision, but I think they could use some financial support. People who have come to the US with me have been making money and sending it back; I'm not. Maybe the family feels sad, but they don't want to say it.

I'm totally torn between my duty to my family and community and my duty to the cause for which I advocate. I'm figuring out that where I go ultimately will be decided by my heart and not my brain.

Hari Acharya has been active in raising international attention and concern for the 97,000 Bhutanese refugees living in camps in Nepal. This unresolved crisis has received little international attention or assistance.

LINKS

www.globalyouthconnect.org

▶ 57.

Human Shield
An Israeli Activist in Palestine

| NETA GOLAN |

▲
Neta Golan

EVELYN HOCKSTEIN

In Israel, Zionism goes without saying. It is the axiom that our society is founded on, and we are taught it is the only remedy for 2,000 years of exile and oppression. In school, we learn how our forefathers were discriminated against and persecuted as a homeless minority. Sometimes, old people with numbers branded into their arms would come and talk to us. The world was scary but simple. There were good guys and there were bad guys. And of course, we were the good guys.

I was about 15 when I first heard about the occupied territories (at that time they used to call them Judea and Sumeria). I must have been there several times, but when a young woman explained that there were people who were living under military rule without basic civil rights in my country, I was shocked. I recall an argument I had with an older boy at school when I was talking about the horrible terrorists that blow up buses. He asked me what the difference is between someone blowing up a bus and a Phantom Jet bombing a refugee camp? I answered that Israeli Phantom Jets never bombed refugee camps. When I got home I asked my father if we ever did. He said that the terrorists thought that if they hid in the refugee camps, they could attack us. To this day in Israel, Palestinian fighters are always called terrorists — even when they are attacking soldiers.

December 17, 2000

Hares is a beautiful West Bank village that has become my home for the last month. Ancient olive trees — more than 1,500 of them — have been cut down or uprooted in the past two months by the Israeli army. Now Israeli settlers surround the village. As with many other Palestinian villages, Hares has been under siege from the beginning of the Intifada. Its inhabitants have been denied the right to move in or out, to go to work, to receive medical treatment, or to study.

Today, I've joined the villagers in opening and removing a roadblock. We're trying to lift the cement block, placed at the village entrance by the Israeli army, with crowbars. The heavy men are standing on the bars. I am sticking stones under the lifted block and the rest of us are pushing.

My presence is meant to reduce the chances that the passing army patrols will open fire on us. It is a terrifying reality that Palestinian/Arab blood does not count for much in the world these days. If anyone bothers to ask questions about why people are killed, the army can always claim that the people were throwing stones, as if that is a good enough reason for killing someone. When Israeli or foreign people and cameras are present, the army's behavior is usually more restrained: shooting an Israeli girl could lose someone a vote.

We push the cement block for about an hour, until it finally rolls over. It is a small victory in the face of an impending catastrophe. We know that the army can put many more blocks whenever they are ordered to and that thousands of villages in the West Bank and Gaza remain under siege, but we allow ourselves to enjoy it for the moment.

When I arrive home to the family that is hosting me, I get a call from my friend Ata Jaber. Ata and his family are farmers from the Baka Valley, near Hebron. He tells me that his house has been taken over by Israeli settlers. The police have notified the family that settlers will be allowed to stay until after Shabbat. If Palestinians attempt to take over a settler house they would be shot dead within minutes.

Ata's house has been demolished twice in the past, on the grounds that he built it without a permit. But Palestinians in the Israeli-controlled occupied territories are not given building permits! My heart is breaking. I am familiar with the process. I need to break down every once in a while, allow myself to be devastated. And then, somehow, I get up stronger. Now I know I need to be with the Jabers.

Because it is a Friday evening, Palestinian cars cannot travel on the main roads, and now even the side roads are blocked. The settler buses don't run until Saturday evening because of Shabbat, so my friend Maxine and I decide to hitch a ride with settlers to Tel Aviv and then continue via Jerusalem to Hebron. On the way, the very polite South African Jewish immigrants who pick us up explain that a burned car on the side of the road was destroyed by Israeli settlers who feel that the army is doing nothing to protect them. Maxine and I swallow hard. I smile at the little girl sitting next to me and feel the crack in my heart deepening.

We arrive in Tel Aviv. The nonstop city people are crowding the restaurants on this wintry weekend, so near and yet so far from the reality of the occupation just around the corner. There is a lot they don't know and don't bother to find out.

The Israeli media, like the Palestinian media, show only one side of the picture. When Jews are hurt or killed, they are always

CONTEXT

exposed in their humanness. They are named: mothers wives, husbands, and children. If Palestinians are killed, the Israeli media usually just give the number of people or terrorists or rioters killed. Even when those killed are children, the focus is skewed.

"They are sending their children to die," is all one has to hear to avoid realizing that we are killing them. The major newspapers don't bother to explain that some die on their way from school or even in their homes. The number of Palestinian dead has reached at least 323 (80 of them children); 10,500 have been wounded. Jewish casualties are 33 dead and 390 injured. Yet many Jews still feel as if they are victims of a vicious attack. The Palestinians are not perceived as an occupied people fighting for their freedom but as a group of bloodthirsty savages out to exterminate the Jews.

I get a minibus to Jerusalem. On the way, an Army head honcho is talking on a radio talk show. He believes the solution to the conflict is political but says, "First things first. We must win the current battle." He advises using maximum force; anything else, in his opinion, "would be interpreted by the other side as weakness and not as an expression of our superior morals, which they do not understand." A news bulletin says that a 13-year-old boy from the Jaber family has been shot. Is this really happening?

There is a wise saying that you become what you hate. My people have gone so far to make sure that the holocaust never happens to us again that we are not aware that we have become racist and elitist and indifferent to our brothers' and sisters' suffering, just like those that made us suffer.

ANOTHER VOICE

Maybe I cannot change narrow-minded thinking. Maybe I cannot broaden a thousand ways of thinking or a hundred, but at least I can broaden one. And I hope one way will broaden another and another and one more, until what we believe will not destroy us anymore.

— Mercy Fajarina

It has taken many years for me to be able to feel as safe as I do with my Palestinian family. I have had to work through the immense fear that I was conditioned with. Whenever I got on the Palestinian minibus that took me to the West Bank, I was terrified. The beginning of the journey was always hell, and then slowly the reality would sink in: these are people sitting beside me — on their way home, on their way to work. Beautiful people. Each time, I knew my fear was getting a little bit weaker. Now, years later, my fear comes up only in crisis situations. And fear and I have become friends now; I can welcome it, knowing that when the wave passes I will see things more clearly. It is the same as my despair. If I just let it through, it makes me stronger.

We arrive in Jerusalem. I have a few hours to pass until after Shabbat, when I can catch the settler bus to Hebron. There is an incredible rainbow above the old city. I remember the Old Testament story that the rainbow is a sign of God's promise to Noah that he would never destroy the world again. The story and the beauty of the rainbow comfort me.

The myth that the Jews are somehow morally superior to the Arabs was rooted in me, as in every Israeli child. When I attended a group to which both Jewish Israeli and Palestinian Israeli women belonged, I exposed this belief to my Palestinian friends. It was very difficult, but I knew that if I wanted to really examine my beliefs, I needed to put them out in the open. So I told them that deep inside I believed that they were crueler than we were. That if the Arabs had won the war, all the Jews would have been killed.

I think that the shock on their faces spoke more than their words. They replied that there had always been Jews living in

Palestine. And before it became clear that the Jews wanted to take over, the relationships had always been good. They thought that if the Arabs had won, we could all live here.

For Israelis, 1948 was the year when people danced in the streets. The United Nations decided on the Partition in Palestine and Israel declared independence. I was told that in the war that followed we were solely defending ourselves and were victorious. I learned slowly that for my Palestinian friends, 1948 was the year of the *nakba*, the catastrophe. A year in which they underwent massacres and in which a million refugees were forced to leave their homes and (as of now) never return. For them, it was a year of exile, hunger, and poverty. From then on, it became difficult for me to celebrate Independence Day. I couldn't celebrate our victory and their tragedy. Although my fear was not uprooted, both perspectives broadened everyone's ability to understand and see each other better. It was healing for all of us — a place to start.

I believe deeply that a conflict can only really be solved when both sides in the conflict are happy and safe. That is real victory. My father shares a view with many Israelis that supporting Palestinians means betraying my people. I do not think that that is the case. I believe that for Jews to be safe and free, Palestinians need to have safety and freedom. Otherwise we are preparing our children for a legacy of war. So I am working on our joint interest — peace and justice — which is a requirement for all of us and for all of our children.

▼

Neta Golan is a Jewish peace activist who has turned herself into a human shield to protect Palestinian olive growers in Hares. A therapist specializing in Chinese medicine, she is part of a small but growing number of Israelis who have been horrified by the Palestinian death toll since the start of the Intifada.

▶ 58.

Love

What the Activist World Needs Now

| TSIPI MANKOVSKY |

Tsipi Mankovsky

COURTESY OF TSIPI MANKOVSKY

I believe I became an activist the first time I asked myself: Why? I've always been an observer. I remember being really little at family celebrations and holidays. When dinner was over, all of the other kids at the table went to play. I never joined them, choosing instead to remain at the table, a small figure in an oversized chair, listening. I soaked up the discussion with a quiet intensity and stayed away from anything that would keep me from hearing any after-dinner revelations. After a while, I could hear other conversations surfacing. I learned to hear all of the things that were never said. I learned to feel the rise and fall of various emotions, and I could pick up on the more subtle arguments. To this day, observation remains my most powerful form of activism. It is my anchor, my solace, and my most powerful tool in challenging and confronting assumptions.

Observation has allowed me to meet different aspects of myself and to develop tolerance and curiosity. That has led me to a deeper understanding and questioning of the world.

✌

I believe that activism in its purest form is about expressing a hope that has not yet found a voice. It is about inspiring a more compelling vision of what already is. I am continuously challenged by the concept of activism and what it means to activate. Many times I have had to abandon my assumptions of what activism *should* look like.

The image most of us conjure up when we hear the word "activist" is that of an angry individual chaining herself to a tree, defying a seething bulldozer. That kind of commitment is admirable but it also creates a narrow definition of what it means to be an activist.

Here's another thought: Maybe there will come a day when the concept of activism will seem like a ridiculous notion. Maybe our great-great-grandchildren will one day exclaim: You mean people had to fight to be heard? You mean, not everyone felt empowered? Maybe when we get better at realizing that when you share power, there is more to go around, we will see the end of activism as we now know it.

✌

My sister and I were riding the subway from downtown back to our home. We were in a silly mood and decided to shake things up a bit, so we asked each other: How can we spread the love? We got out our markers and notepads and made a sign that proudly read: "Love train." We jumped to the front car and pressed the sign against the front window. As the train approached each station, the sign was visible to everyone on the platform. Every time we got a smile from someone, we knew the world had changed in a subtle yet profound way. We knew this by the way our hearts felt: light and open.

In Toronto, people are usually really quiet on the trains. Strangers don't often strike up conversation and people tend to keep to themselves. So it was nice to get the whole train smiling! As we neared the end of out trip, a gentleman who caught a glimpse of our sign and laughed, got on. It didn't take long before we were deep in conversation.

ANOTHER **VOICE**

Genuine activism begins as a revolution of heart and mind — a shift in perspective that is liberating in itself. Central to this is the understanding that individual and collective liberation are inseparable. Rather than browbeating people into submission, trying to convince others that you are right and that they must adopt your views, true activism is that which helps others reach their own understanding and through that understanding, freedom.

— Gavin

Tsipi Mankovsky lives in
Toronto, Canada where
she writes for several
publications. She has
attended conferences on
everything from futurism to
child poverty and cocreated
a website called Coolgirls,
a feminist website for
young women.

LINKS

www.coolgirls.org

We discovered that we would be taking the same bus. We chatted about jobs, school, and love. He was telling us about his girlfriend and his plans to marry her. "Relationships are all about trust and communication," he told us. We all parted feeling good; it was a good night. We still see him sometimes — he's a waiter at a restaurant near our home. The thing is that in a big city like Toronto, you build community wherever you find yourself — even if that's on the subway going home.

I am one person in a world of six billion. So, am I important? I want to believe that I am. I want to believe that my life is a gift to the world, that I can change the things that stop us from seeing each other as real, whole people. It is not easy to believe in yourself and believe you can make a difference. Let's face it, the toughest part about this gig is having faith in yourself (never mind the world!). I have proven to myself over and over again that, whatever it is I'm trying to do, I can!

I still sometimes doubt, hesitate, and shy away from challenges. But that's also part of the joy — going for it anyway. When I see myself going beyond what I thought was possible, it spills over into the world. "My cup runneth over." This ain't no joke folks! — it's inevitable. The cool thing about love is that it gets even stronger and even sweeter when you share it.

In those moments when my mind becomes calm and still, I hear my soul say: Tsipora, the world doesn't need to be saved; it just needs to be loved. At the core of my being, I believe that each one of us has something really special, something really magical to bring to the world. I've seen what happens when I learn to love the stranger — the friend and the foe. I've learned that love is stronger; it is the most potent of powers. And it is love that changes the world.

▶ 59.

YES!

Activism at the Speed of Life

| TAD HARGRAVE |

▲

Tad Hargrave

Judging by the pace of activism today, I wouldn't be surprised if tomorrow I see people like Han Shan (the director of programs for Ruckus Society) begging for change in the Safeway parking lot, with a sign saying: "Burned out activist. Will lockdown for food."

Let's face it, we're all very busy and the movement can get pretty *yang*, if you know what I mean. Sometimes the feminine qualities of simply resting, holding space, and nourishing relationships can be left by the wayside. Those of us in the movement could probably stand to take the advice of the bumper sticker I saw recently: "Don't just do something. Sit there!"

Youth for Environmental Sanity (YES!), the organization I work for, has been focusing on addressing the burnout and isolation many young activists feel. And, if there's a magic potion for that, it's one word: community. Building community by building bridges of trust; building trust by creating safe space.

Safe space is created when people in a group agree to listen and share deeply without judgment; when they know that whatever they say will be kept within the group; when they can trust they won't be attacked for whatever they contribute; and when diversity is

celebrated and every tactic is welcomed. This often gets left out of the movement by default, yet we work together much better when we feel safe, embraced, and accepted.

At YES!, we hold annual Youth Leadership JAMS!, which bring together 30 leading global youth activists for seven days of community building, skills sharing, rest, and celebration. YES JAMS! are not designed as a forum for discussing pressing activist issues. They aren't summits, symposiums, inform- ation exchanges, conferences, camps, gatherings, sessions, or convergences. They are JAMS!

We always begin our JAMS! by telling participants that we didn't bring them together to have them create the Super Network or to write up a manifesto from the youth of the world. We tell them we didn't even bring them to collaborate with each other. We brought them because we think they are not only 30 of the most awesome young activists we know, but also 30 of the most stressed young activists we know. For a week, we encourage them to take space, chill out, breathe. We tell them to get to know each other professionally and fall in love with each other as people, and that miracles will happen. And they do. Consistently.

We have found, again and again, that there is a power in coming together to do nothing but hang out and build relationships.

Participants at Yes! Jam 2000

It's covert activism. It's building deep foundations. It's pausing to let the roots of our activism sink into the deeper waters that will sustain us. We are human beings, not human doings. The challenges we face in relationships with other activists and coworkers are not preventing the work; they are a part of the work. Environmental legend David Brower knew this well. Each Sunday he would host waffle brunches. They were a regular who's who of the activist world — people just hanging out, building community.

Community shouldn't just happen once a year at a JAM! We need to create it as much as we can where we live, with the people we love and the people we work with. So, here's to more waffle brunches together. This movement will really get somewhere when we remember to move at the speed of life.

Tad Hargrave is the director of international outreach and chief coordinator of YES! (Youth for Environmental Sanity). He is also the founder and trainer for Leaders! International, a youth leadership group that empowers youth to live with passion.

LINKS

www.yesworld.org

▶ 60.

Lifelong Activism
Finding the Courage, Tenacity, and Love

| STARHAWK |

▲
Starhawk

THE PROTEST AGAINST THE G8, GENOA, JULY 2001

Thursday:

The French students are noisy — laughing, arguing, leaping and pummeling each other in the role plays we do as part of our direct action training. They are tall, lean, as full of vitality as a pack of young gazelles. "The French are strong," we tell them, as they pull each other out of a blockade form no other group has been able to break. I am in love with all of them.

Friday:

We are together in the Pink Bloc — the cluster that wants to go through the action dancing, drumming, bringing laughter and frivolity to a war zone. One of the French women climbs the fence that the police have erected to protect most of inner Genoa from the presence of protesters. Police fire a water cannon and she is knocked off. She springs back up, laughing.

Tear gas canisters arc over our heads and the square fills with noxious fumes. Drumming and laughing, we begin a retreat to a safe space, the square where the women's groups and pacifist religious networks have gathered. As we try to decide what to do next, massive amounts of tear gas cloud the air. We scatter. I find some of my Pink friends in an alley. We regroup, cross the main street, and head up the stairways of Genoa's old town, only a minute ahead of the riot cops who are savagely beating people. Vincent, one of the French students, is hit on the head so badly that they take him to the hospital.

Saturday:

In the morning, I see Vincent at the clinic in the Indymedia Center (IMC) building. His head swollen to twice its normal size, he looks like a character from Star Trek. He had been arrested at the hospital. In the police station, they had pulled his arms up behind his back and smashed his wounded head down on a table, over and over again, for hours. He is upset because they have taken his papers, and so he cannot go to the big march. "The French are strong," we tell him. "They have to be."

On Saturday night, the Pink Bloc has just finished a meeting at the IMC when the police attack. Our building is spared, but only because a member of the European Parliament is present. Across the street, police enter the Diaz school where people are sleeping and beat them senseless. They break bones, shatter teeth, smash skulls. For hours we watch while the stretchers are being carried out. I'll never know which of the hundreds of young people I've met are now lying broken or are being marched away to be tortured in rooms with pictures of Mussolini and pornography on the walls. It is amazing, awe-inspiring, and sometimes heartbreaking to witness the courage of these frontline activists.

SEATTLE, GENOA AND BEYOND

Before Seattle, most people had no idea what direct action in the streets is all about. The events during the Seattle protests, and the mass mobilizations since, have changed the political landscape of our times. It can be very powerful and can transform the rage and anger that frontline activists often feel.

But direct action is not the only kind of political action that is needed. Calling government agencies, writing letters to legislators, knocking on doors, finding out who's filed a timber harvest claim — all that stuff is the daily, ongoing, nonstop, often boring grind of political action. You don't get the adrenaline rush of the big mobilizations. But it is really important work. Movements take time, persistence, and longevity, as well as passion and raw action.

Ultimately, you've got to find something that you love so much you're not only willing to put your life on the line for it, you're also able to draw some sustenance from it. Youth all over the world have visions of what the world could be, and they're learning the skills to make it so. They are running anarchist cafés and planting gardens. Organizing ecology groups at conservative colleges and learning how to retrofit trucks to run on vegetable oil. Like their counterparts who go to action after action, these activists resist the global economic system and the ongoing forces that aim to stifle dissent. They amaze me with their courage, their resilience, and their matter-of-fact acceptance of the struggle.

The youth are strong. They have to be.

Starhawk is an author and feminist and has been an activist for over 30 years. She lives part-time in San Francisco, where she works with Reclaiming, a community that offers classes, intensives, and public rituals in the tradition of Witchcraft.

LINKS

www.riseup.net/rant

Epilogue

We could never have imagined that, the day after completing this book, the world would change so dramatically. Words cannot describe the emotions we felt as we watched in horror the crisis of September 11, 2001. Like millions of people worldwide, we join in mourning the loss of so many lives.

The attacks on the World Trade Center and the Pentagon have thrust us into a new era of uncertainty. In response, the IMF and World Bank have cancelled their September 2001 meetings in Washington, DC and the WTO meeting scheduled for Qatar in November 2001 has become tentative.

The call for peace and justice has become all the more urgent. Activists are joining countless others around the world to urge restraint in the use of military retaliation against terrorism. They are highlighting the connection between the violence of the West's economic, military, and foreign policies and the growing anger, fear, and desperation of oppressed people.

Now, more than ever, we must examine the consequences of our denial, ignorance, and complacency. We must strive to better understand world history, religious beliefs, cultural diversity, and the impact of ideologies and policies that oppress and marginalize people. Terror is still terror, no matter what its origin: whether it stems from a sudden, deliberate act or is visited every day upon a people through poverty, starvation, environmental destruction, economic enslavement, or police or military brutality.

But we need to go further than an examination of consequences. We need to acknowledge our common humanity: our mutual right to the basics of life — food, water, and shelter; our desire for healthcare, education, and self-determination; our hopes for our children; our need for love; and our desire for peace. Extremists of any kind will always be a threat. Our work is to continue to hold the vision of a just and beautiful world. In solidarity we can choose to embody compassion, tolerance, forgiveness, understanding, and love.

OCTOBER 1, 2001

We must not be afraid of dreaming the seemingly impossible
— if we want the seemingly impossible to become a reality.
— Václav Havel

Resources

Resources are everywhere! Here are a select few that we came across as we researched stories, organizations, and issues for the book. Each listing is a window into many more valuable resources. Seek and you shall find!

ACTIVISM/ORGANIZING

Action Center
www.actionpa.org
215-743-4884

Activism 2000 Project
www.youthactivism.com
1-800-Kid-Power

Center for Campus Organizing
www.cco.org
617-725-2886

Center for Environmental Citizenship
www.envirocitizen.org
202-547-8435

Direct Action Network
www.directactionnetwork.org
PO Box 1485,
Asheville NC, 28802 USA

Global Youth Action Network
www.Youthlink.org
212-661-6111

Protest.Net
www.protest.net

Refuse and Resist
www.refuseandresist.org
212-713-5657

ALTERNATIVE MEDIA

Internet

Alternet
www.alternet.org
415-284-1420

Cubafacts.com
www.cubafacts.com

Direct Action Media Network
http://damn.tao.ca
215-386-8835

Disinformation
www.disinfo.com

Earth First! Journal
www.earthfirstjournal.org/index.html
520-620-6900 (voice)

Guardian Unlimited, UK
www.guardian.co.uk
020 7278 2332

Independent Media Center
(links to international Indy
Media Centers)
www.indymedia.org
206-262-0721

Media Island
www.mediaisland.org
360-352-8526

Oneworld.net
www.oneworld.org

Reporteros Sin Fronteras/Reporters
without Borders
http://www.rsf.fr

Webactive
www.webactive.com
Fax: 206-674-2696

Znet (or *Z Magazine*)
www.zmag.org
18 Millfield Street,
Woods Hole, MA 02543 USA

Video

Free Speech TV
www.freespeech.org
PO Box 6060,
Boulder, CO 80306 USA

Headwaters Action Video Collective
www.havc.org
415-820-1635

Paper Tiger
www.papertiger.org
212-420-9045

Whispered Media
www.whisperedmedia.org
415-789-8484

Youth Media Network

LA Youth
www.layouth.com
5967 W. Third Street, Suite 301
Los Angeles CA 90036 USA

Listen Up!
www.pbs.org/merrow/trt
212-725-7000

New Youth Connections
www.youthcomm.org/Publications/
NYC.htm
212-279-0708

Youth Outlook
www.youthoutlook.org
415-438-4755

Wiretap
www.wiretap.org
415-284-1420

In print

Adbusters magazine (and online)
www.epinet.org
800-663-1243 worldwide

Colorlines
www.arc.org
510-653-3415

Corporate Watch
www.corpwatch.org
415-561-6568

Multinational Monitor
www.essential.org/monitor
202-387-8030

On the Air

Alternative Radio
www.alternativeradio.org
800-444-1977

New Dimensions Radio
www.newdimensions.org
707-468-5215

RESOURCES

Organizations

Fairness and Accuracy in Reporting (FAIR)
⊟ www.fair.org
☎ 212-633-6700

Institute for Public Accuracy
⊟ www.accuracy.org
☎ 415-552-5378

Media Alliance
⊟ www.media-alliance.org
☎ 415-546-6334

One World
⊟ www.oneworld.net
☎ 202-638-5770

Video Activist Network
⊟ www.videoactivism.org
☎ 415- 789-8484

We Interrupt This Message
⊟ www.interrupt.org
☎ 415-537-9437
☎ 212-694-1144

ANIMAL RIGHTS

Alliance for Animals
⊟ www.allanimals.org
☎ 608-257-6333

Animal Liberation Frontline
Information Service
⊟ www.animalliberation.net

Animal Welfare Institute
⊟ www.awionline.org
☎ 202-337-2332

Last Chance For Animals
⊟ www.lcanimal.org
☎ 310-271-6096

No Compromise
⊟ www.nocompromise.org
☎ 831-425-3007

People for the Ethical Treatment of
Animals
⊟ www.peta-online.org
☎ 757-622-7382

The Jane Goodall Institute
⊟ www.janegoodall.org
☎ 301-565-0086

The Sea Shepherd
Conservation Society
⊟ www.seashepherd.org
Fax: 310-456-2488

Vegan Action
⊟ www.vegan.org

ANARCHISM

Anarchist Yellow Pages
⊟ www.flag.blackened.net/agony/ayp.htm

An Anarchy Home Page
⊟ www.andrew.cmu.edu/~ctb/anarchy

Institute for Anarchist Studies
⊟ www.flag.blackened.net/ias/

Anarchist Action Network
⊟ www.zpub.com/notes/aadl.html

CYBER ACTIVISM

Anarchist Infoshop
⊟ www.infoshop.org

Zapatistas in Cyberspace
⊟ www.eco.utexas.edu/Homepages/Faculty/Cleaver/zapsincyber.html

DEMOCRACY

Alliance for Democracy
⊟ www.afd-online.org
☎ 781-894-1179

Center for Living Democracy
⊟ www.livingdemocracy.org
☎ 802-254-1234

Common Cause
⊟ www.commoncause.org
☎ 202-833-1200

The Center for Responsive Politics
⊟ www.opensecrets.org
☎ 202-857-0044

Public Campaign
⊟ www.publiccampaign.org
☎ 202-293-0222

Reclaim Democracy!
⊟ www.reclaimdemocracy.org
☎ 303-402-0105

The Center for Voting and Democracy
⊟ www.igc.apc.org/cvd/
☎ 301-270-4616

180 Degree Movement for Democracy
⊟ www.corporations.org/democracy
☎ 608-262-9036

EDUCATION

Commercial Alert
⊟ www.commercialalert.org
☎ 503-235-8012

The Institute for Earth Education
⊟ www.earthed.com/default.asp
☎ 304-832-6404

The Center for Commercial-Free
Public Education
⊟ www.commercialfree.org
☎ 415-241-6493

Power to the Youth
⊟ www.youthpower.net
615 Little Silver Point Road,
Little Silver, NJ 07739 USA

ENVIRONMENTAL

Aseed
⊟ www.aseed.net
PO Box 92066,
1090 AB Amsterdam,
The Netherlands
☎ +31-20-668-2236

Bioneers
⊟ www.bioneers.org
☎ 877-246-6337 (toll free)

Earth Island Institute
⊟ www.earthisland.org
☎ 415-788-3666

Earth Liberation Front
⊟ www.earthliberationfront.com
☎ 503-478-0902

Friends of the Earth
⊟ www.foe.org
☎ 202-783-7400

Greenpeace International
⊟ www.greenpeace.org
☎ 202-462-1177

International Rivers Network
⊟ www.irn.org
☎ 510-848-1155

Native Forest Council
⊟ www.forestcouncil.org
☎ 541-688-2600

Rainforest Action Network
🖥 www.ran.org .
☎ 415-398-4404

Sierra Club
🖥 www.sierraclub.org
☎ 415-977-5500

Institute for Local Self-Reliance
🖥 www.ilsr.org
☎ 612-379-3815

The White Earthland Recovery Project
🖥 www.welrp.org/index.html
☎ 888-779-3577

Worldwatch Institute
🖥 www.worldwatch.org
☎ 202-452-1999

FEMINIST/WOMEN'S ISSUES

Arab Women's Solidarity Association
🖥 www.awsa.net

Feminist.com
🖥 www.feminist.com
☎ 212-396-0262

Feminist Majority Foundation
🖥 www.feminist.org
☎ 703-522-2214

National Organization for Women
🖥 www.now.org
☎ 202-628-8669

Radical Women
🖥 www.socialism.com
☎ 206-722-6057

Solidarity
🖥 www.igc.org/solidarity
☎ 313-841-0160

The Daughters Sisters Project
🖥 www.daughters-sisters.org
☎ 206-842-3000

The Images of Divinity Project
🖥 www.imagesofdivinity.org

Third Wave
🖥 www.thirdwavefoundation.org
☎ 212-388-1898

Violence Against Women Office
🖥 www.ojp.usdoj.gov/vawo/about.htm
☎ 202-307-6026

Women's Edge
🖥 www.womensedge.org
☎ 202-884 8396

FOOD AND FARMS

Bioengineering Action Network
🖥 www.tao.ca/~ban

Corporate Agribusiness
Research Project
🖥 home.earthlink.net/~avkrebs/CARP/
☎ 703-461-3393

Institute for Agriculture
and Trade Policy
🖥 www.ifg.org/ifa
☎ 612-379-5980

Redefining Progress
🖥 www.rprogress.org
☎ 510-444-3041

True Food Network
🖥 www.truefoodnow.org

The Organic Consumers Association
🖥 www.purefood.org
☎ 218- 226-4164

GAY RIGHTS

Act Up
🖥 www.actupny.org
☎ 212-966-4873

Gay, Lesbian, and Straight Education
Network
🖥 www.glsen.org
☎ 212-727-0135

International Lesbian and Gay
Association, Brussels
🖥 www.ilga.org
☎ +32-2-5022471

Queer War Society
🖥 www.geocities.com/CapitolHill/
Lobby/6371/index.html

GLOBALIZATION
ECONOMIC JUSTICE

50 Years Is Enough
🖥 www.50years.org
☎ 202-463-2265

Economic Policy Institute
🖥 www.epinet.org
☎ 202-775-8810

International Forum on Globalization
🖥 www.ifg.org
☎ 415-561-7650

Jubilee USA Network
🖥 www.j2000usa.org
☎ 202-783-3566

Oxfam International
🖥 www.oxfam.org
☎ 617 482 1211

Public Citizen
🖥 www.citizen.org
☎ 800-289-3787

The World Revolution
🖥 www.worldrevolution.org

United for a Fair Economy
🖥 www.ufenet.org
☎ 617-423-2148

HUMAN, LABOR
AND CIVIL RIGHTS

AFL-CIO
🖥 www.aflcio.org
☎ 202-639-5000

Amnesty International
🖥 www.amnesty.org
☎ 212-807-8400

Defending Those Who Give
the Earth a Voice
🖥 www.defendtheearth.org

Ella Baker Center for Human Rights
🖥 www.ellabakercenter.org
☎ 415-951-4844

Forefront
🖥 www.forefrontleaders.org
☎ 212-845-5273

Free Mumia
🖥 www.freemumia.org
☎ 415-695-7745

Free the Children
🖥 www.freethechildren.org
☎ 905-760-9382

Jobs with Justice
🖥 www.jwj.org
☎ 202-434-1106

Homes Not Jails
🖥 www.homesnotjails.org

Human Rights Watch
⊟ www.hrw.org
(212-290-4700

Indigenous and Non-Indigenous
Youth Alliance
⊟ www.agamanawa.com/iniya.html
(510-547-2270

NAACP (National Association for the
Advancement of Colored People)
⊟ www.naacp.org
(410-358-8900

National Labor Committee
⊟ www.nlcnet.org
(212-242-3002

National Network for Immigrant and
Refugee Rights
⊟ www.nnirr.org
(510-465-1885

People and Planet, UK
⊟ www.peopleandplanet.org

Project Underground
⊟ www.moles.org
(510-705-8981

Students Committee Against Labor
Exploitation
⊟ www.nlcnet.org
(212-242-3002

Sweatshop Watch
⊟ www.sweatshopwatch.org
(510-834-8990

INDIGENOUS RIGHTS

Amanaka'a Amazon Network
⊟ www.amanakaa.org

Indigiaction
⊟ www.indigenous.gibsonnet.net

Lakota Student Alliance
⊟ www.dickshovel.com/lsa.html
(605-867-1507

NAWA Institute
⊟ www.agamanawa.com

Survival for Tribal Peoples
⊟ www.survival.org

PEACE, NONVIOLENCE, ANTIWAR, AND ANTI-MILITARISM

Associations of World Citizens
⊟ www.worldcitizens.org
(415-541-9610

End the Arms Race
⊟ www.peacewire.org
(604-687-3223

Fellowship of Reconciliation
⊟ www.nonviolence.org/for
(845-358-4601

Food not Bombs
⊟ www.foodnotbombs.net
(800-884-1136

Global Peace Campaign
⊟ www.peace2001.org

Ground Zero
⊟ www.gzcenter.org
(360-377-2586

International Campaign to Ban Landmines
⊟ www.icbl.org
(202-547-2667

MidEast Citizen Diplomacy
⊟ www.mideastdiplomacy.org
(360-297-2280

Peace Action
⊟ www.peace-action.org
(202-862-9740

Peace, Inc.
⊟ www.peaceinc.org
(501-283-9050

Seeds of Peace
⊟ www.seedsofpeace.org
(212-573-8040

Student Peace Action Network
⊟ www.gospan.org
(202-862-9762

The International Youth Co-operation
⊟ www.iyoco.org
(831-643-0775

The Nonviolence Web
⊟ www.nonviolence.org
PO Box 30947,
Philadelphia, PA 19104 USA

War Resisters League
⊟ www.warresisters.org
(212- 228-0450

PRISON INDUSTRIAL COMPLEX/ ANTI-RACISM

October 22 Coalition
⊟ www.october22.org
(888-NO BRUTALITY

Prison Activist Resource Center
⊟ www.prisonactivist.org
(510-893-4648

Prison Moratorium Project
⊟ www.nomoreprisons.org
(510-893-4648 ext 202

STUDENT GROUPS

Young Democratic Socialists
⊟ www.dsausa.org/youth/youth.htm
(212-727-8610

Public Interest Research Groups
⊟ www.pirg.org/uspirg
(202-546-9707

People and Planet, UK
⊟ www.peopleandplanet.org
((01865) 245678

Student Alliance to Reform Corporations
(STARC)
⊟ www.corpreform.org/home.html
(510-272-9109

Students for a Free Tibet
⊟ www.tibet.org/SFT
(212-358-0071

Students United for a Responsible Global
Environment (SURGE)
⊟ www.unc.edu/surge/main.html
(919-843-6548

Student Environmental Action Coalition
⊟ www.seac.org
(215-222-4711

Youthforce Coalition, CA
(510-444-0484

Neva Welton and Linda Wolf

HEATHER WOLF-SMEETH

About the Authors

LINDA WOLF

A ll my life, I could never keep my mouth shut. In elementary school, it was a problem for my teachers. They would write on my report cards, "Linda speaks out too much." However, it wouldn't be until my teenage years that I would begin speaking out with clear purpose.

In the '50s, my parents would take me to the drive-in and let me play in the children's playground before the movies started. One evening, I was playing with a little boy, when a man walked by and hurled some racist words at him. It was a stunning moment that has haunted me since. Looking back, I think that experience marked the end of my innocence and the beginning of my desire to actively change things that I knew were wrong.

Over the past 40 years, my life as an activist can be mapped. What distinguishes the highest times was the collective nature of working together, struggling for a cause, and no longer feeling so alone and powerless. I was in sympathy with the Civil Rights Movement, protested against the war in Vietnam and the proliferation of nuclear power, and participated in the women's liberation movement. Later, I lived in France, where I learned the fine art of debating and digesting at the same time. Around the table, I developed a deeper analysis of politics and later, as a photographer, to speak out even louder to shake up people's perceptions.

In the '80s I became an earth mother: my daughters had home births, a family bed, and long-term nursing — all revolutionary at the time. As they grew older, I got involved as an activist with them at school, boycotting school testing and convincing the school district to fly an Earth flag and offer vege-burgers as an alternative to meat on the lunch menu.

As my daughters approached the teen years, I recommitted to the women's movement through developing girls' empowerment programs and wrote a book for teenage girls, as much for them as for my own healing. This was a turning point for me. It marked a time when my being an activist no longer stemmed so much from being reactivated but from a deeper, more personal place.

In February 1999, I was invited to attend one of the first Seattle planning meetings for the protest against the WTO. I had never heard of the WTO before. I really didn't know what implications it had on my life or the lives of others. Yet, with each meeting and teach-in I attended, my understanding grew exponentially. I began to see the ways that all the issues I care about intersect with the issues of globalization and the many forms of our current global crises. Participating in the four days of protest was life changing. I don't think any of us was fully prepared for the shock of seeing the response of our government to the concerns of civil society. This has fueled my resolve to stand up and speak out even more against injustice and ignorance and to contribute to creating a vision for a more humane, equitable, loving, and compassionate world. I can't think of anything more important to do with my life.

First and foremost, I am very grateful to Neva for our friendship — what a joy it's been to work with you. I want to deeply thank my beloved mother Barbara Wolf; the father of my children, Tom Smeeth; my families Wolf, Renberg, and Smeeth; and my friends too numerous to name, for supporting me in my process of unfolding. I am especially grateful to my extended family: Libba and Gifford Pinchot, and their children Marianna, Marco, and Alex, whose contributions to me and those I love are incalculable; Lindsay Wagner, Dorian and Ali, Jimmy Mateson, Jean Kilbourne, Leah Green and Peter Hwoschinsky, as well as my family of activists and peacemakers all over the world who, when we meet, feel like we've known each other forever. You are the relationships that sustain me.

Many thanks also to Elisa Romeo and the focus group girls; the Daughters Sisters board, staff, volunteers, and friends; and the many people who have contributed to this project.

Above all, I am deeply grateful to my loving daughters, Heather and Genevieve Wolf-Smeeth, activists in their own right, for whom I am daily motivated to make myself and this world a little more beautiful, tolerant, amusing, and conscious; and to my partner Forrest, for inspiring, enlightening, loving, and supporting me. Without you, Fo, this book would not have been written.

▼

Linda is the cofounder and director of the Daughters Sisters Project, whose mission is to educate, inspire, and empower young women, foster understanding between the genders and generations, and support youth in conscious self-expression and social action. She is the coauthor of the award-winning book Daughters of the Moon, Sisters of the Sun *(New Society Publishers, 1997) and a respected photographer for over 30 years. Her work is collected in museums worldwide, including the Musée het Sterckshof, the Musée Reattu, the Bibliotheque Nationale, and the Smithsonian Institute.*

NEVA WELTON

Like countless others, the WTO protests in November 1999 changed my life forever. All of who I am was called into service after a lifetime of being on the periphery of activist work. In the '60s, I was too young to participate in the anti-Vietnam War protests, but the daily televised reports of the war and the courage and conviction of protesters working for peace and justice left an indelible mark on my psyche.

Indeed, four decades of rich social and political movements, from civil rights and the antiwar movement to women's liberation, gay rights, free speech, consciousness-raising, and environmental activism, shaped my worldview. My values became grounded in freedom, justice, peace, and respect for all living things; and in community and sustainability — despite the influences of a burgeoning corporate culture.

As a young adult, I chose to focus my energies on raising my daughter, living lightly on the planet, being of service to individuals through community work, and paying the bills. I challenged myself to be more responsible for the well-being of Earth and her inhabitants and to find alternative structures to the mainstream paradigm of more, better, faster, now.

Eventually, I earned a Master's degree in Psychology and spent several years working with youth. During that time, I witnessed the crisis of meaning that was pervasive in the lives of young people — a crisis manufactured in large part by the empty values of a toxic popular culture. I became more committed to working to change the systems that bleed the very life out of people and the Earth. I sensed that my true calling was to facilitate transformations — not on an individual basis but as an activist in the 'world channel.'

In September 1999, my daughter went off to college and my daily responsibilities began to shift. Having the WTO stage their trade talks in Seattle was a blessing. It's as if the universe knew that I could finally step fully into activism as a way of life and said: Okay, here's the WTO right in your own backyard.

The rest, as they say, is history. I am a committed activist — organizing, learning, voicing, protesting, writing, and finding as many ways as I know how to be a vehicle for others to get involved. *Global Uprising* is

If you have enjoyed *Global Uprising* you might also enjoy other

BOOKS TO BUILD A NEW SOCIETY

Our books provide positive solutions for people who want to make a difference.
We specialize in:

Nonviolence • Educational and Parenting Resources • Resistance and Community
Sustainable Living • Natural Building & Appropriate Technology
Ecological Design and Planning • New Forestry • Environment and Justice
Conscientious Commerce • Progressive Leadership

For a full list of NSP's titles, please call 1-800-567-6772 or check out our website at:
www.newsociety.com

New Society Publishers

ENVIRONMENTAL BENEFITS STATEMENT

New Society Publishers has chosen to produce this book on New Leaf EcoBook 100, recycled paper made with 100% post consumer waste, processed chlorine free, and old growth free.

For every 5,000 books printed, New Society saves the following resources:[1]

45	Trees
4,049	Pounds of Solid Waste
4,455	Gallons of Water
5,811	Kilowatt Hours of Electricity
7,361	Pounds of Greenhouse Gases
32	Pounds of HAPs, VOCs, and AOX Combined
11	Cubic Yards of Landfill Space

[1]Environmental benefits are calculated based on research done by the Environmental Defense Fund and other members of the Paper Task Force who study the environmental impacts of the paper industry.

For more information on this environmental benefits statement, or to inquire about environmentally friendly papers, please contact New Leaf Paper – info@newleafpaper.com Tel: 888 • 989 • 5323.

NEW SOCIETY PUBLISHERS

very much an expression of my work to build a strong movement for the future of this planet. Being an activist, I've come to believe, isn't something special. As Anita Roddick says, "Activism is the rent we pay to live on the planet."

There are many people to thank for my slow but sure development on the road to being a fully engaged citizen in our so-called democracy. To my wonderful mother, father, and sister, and the rest of the family, who have accepted me as the purple sheep of the family: Happy Solstice, and thank you for your never-ending love and support. To my friends too numerous to name: Thank you for being the foundation that has given me the courage to grow. I am a lucky person to be held with such love in such a wonderful community. To all of the Kitsap Citizen Action Network folks: It is a sincere pleasure to massage the constant challenge of activism and social transformation with all of you. To my coauthor Linda, who has opened doors for me and continually teaches me to be a Yes! person: Thank you for the grace of a co-creative project well done. To the many contributors to *Global Uprising*, both published and unpublished: It has been a great honor to connect with each of you. I have learned as much as I can from your experiences and wisdom and vow to hold each of your stories with reverence as we go out into the world to promote the book. To my daughter Carla: Thank you for your support and love and for letting me constantly ply you with worldly information. May your life and the life of your children and their children and onward be blessed with ancient forests, clean air and water, freedom, respect, equality, love, and justice for all. It is, after all, one of the big reasons why I do what I do.

Neva has a Master's degree in Counseling Psychology. She has worked with youth through community mental health programs, private practice, and nonprofit organizations. She facilitates groups in Rites of Passage journeys through the Institute for Cultural Affairs and works with the Daughters Sisters Project, facilitating workshops for adults and young women. Currently, she devotes her energy to social transformation, as a community organizer, activist, and writer. She is cofounder of Kitsap Citizen Action Network, a grassroots activist organization.